# Kaleidoscope
# Coloring Mandalas

*Copyright: Published in the United States by Peter Raymond*
*Published July 2018*
*ISBN-13: 978-1722275853*
*ISBN-10: 1722275855*

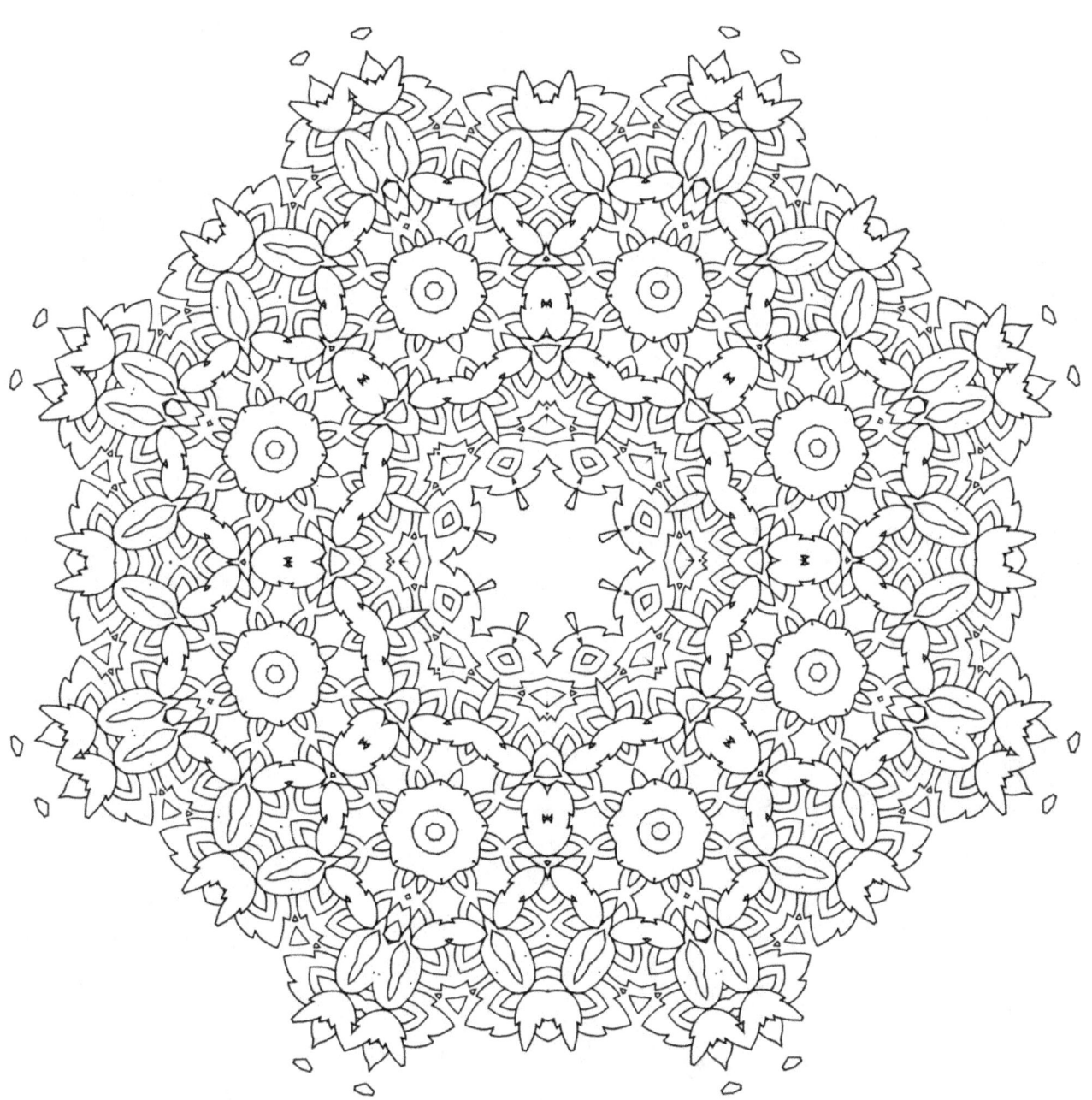

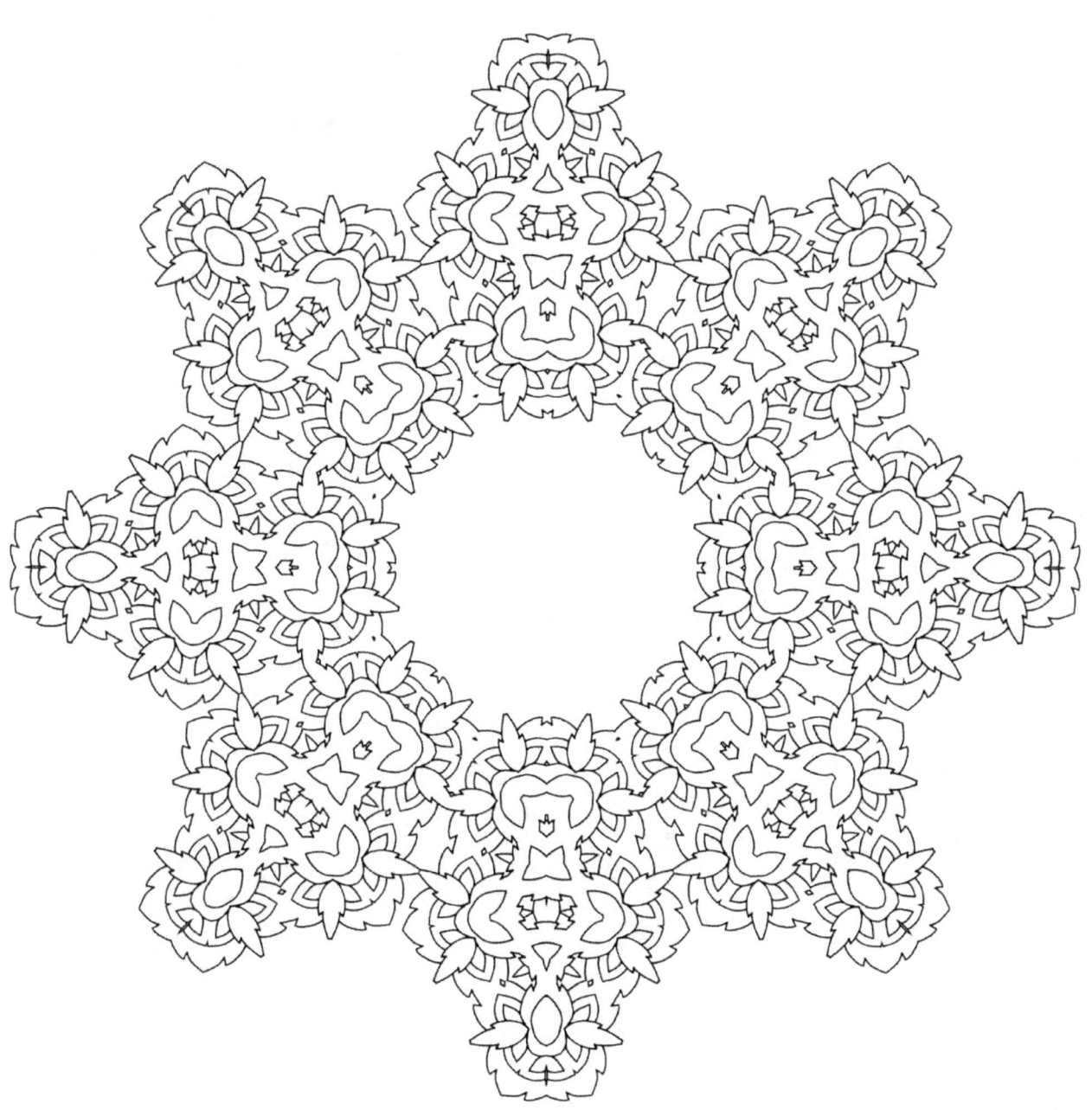

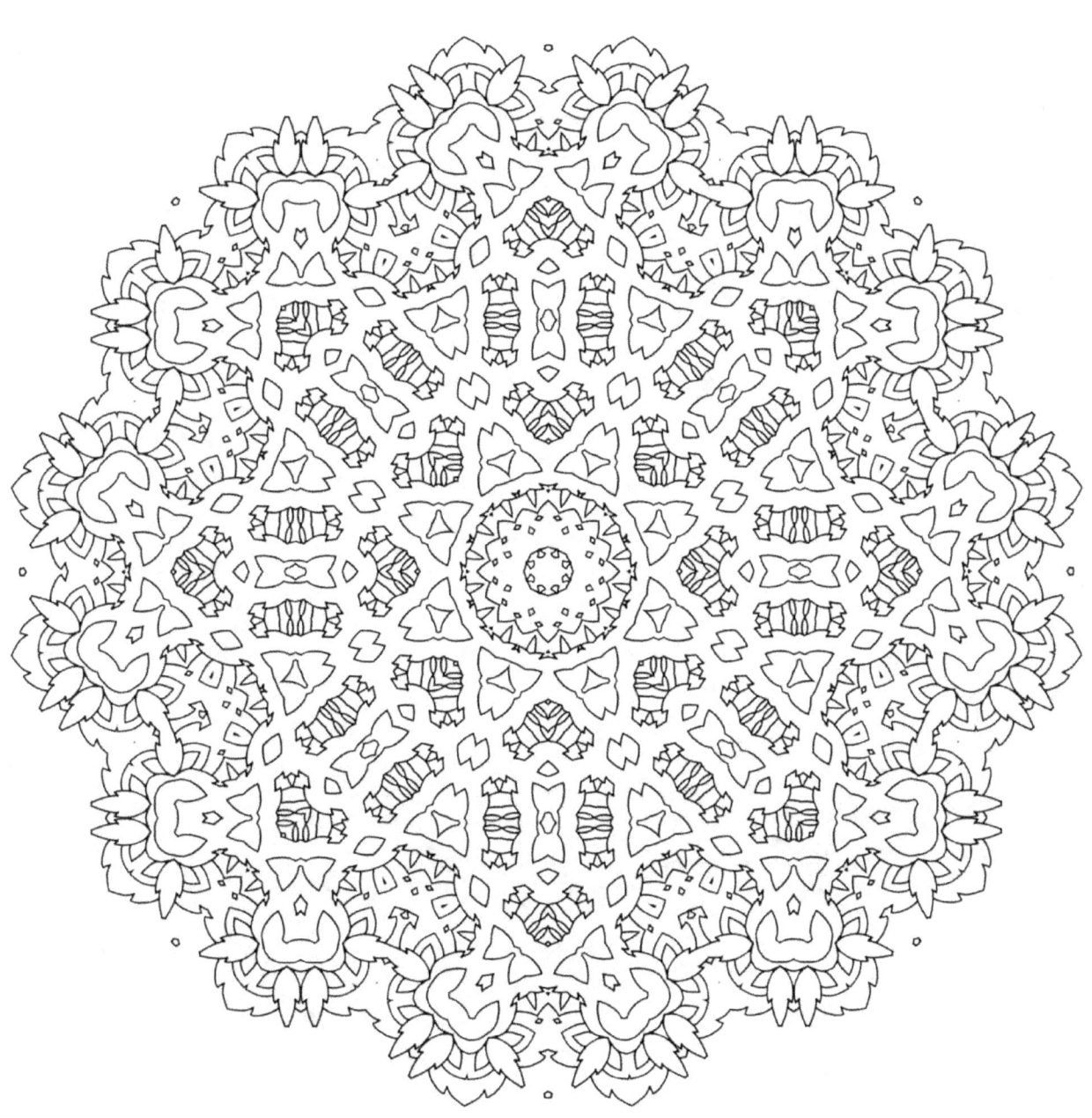

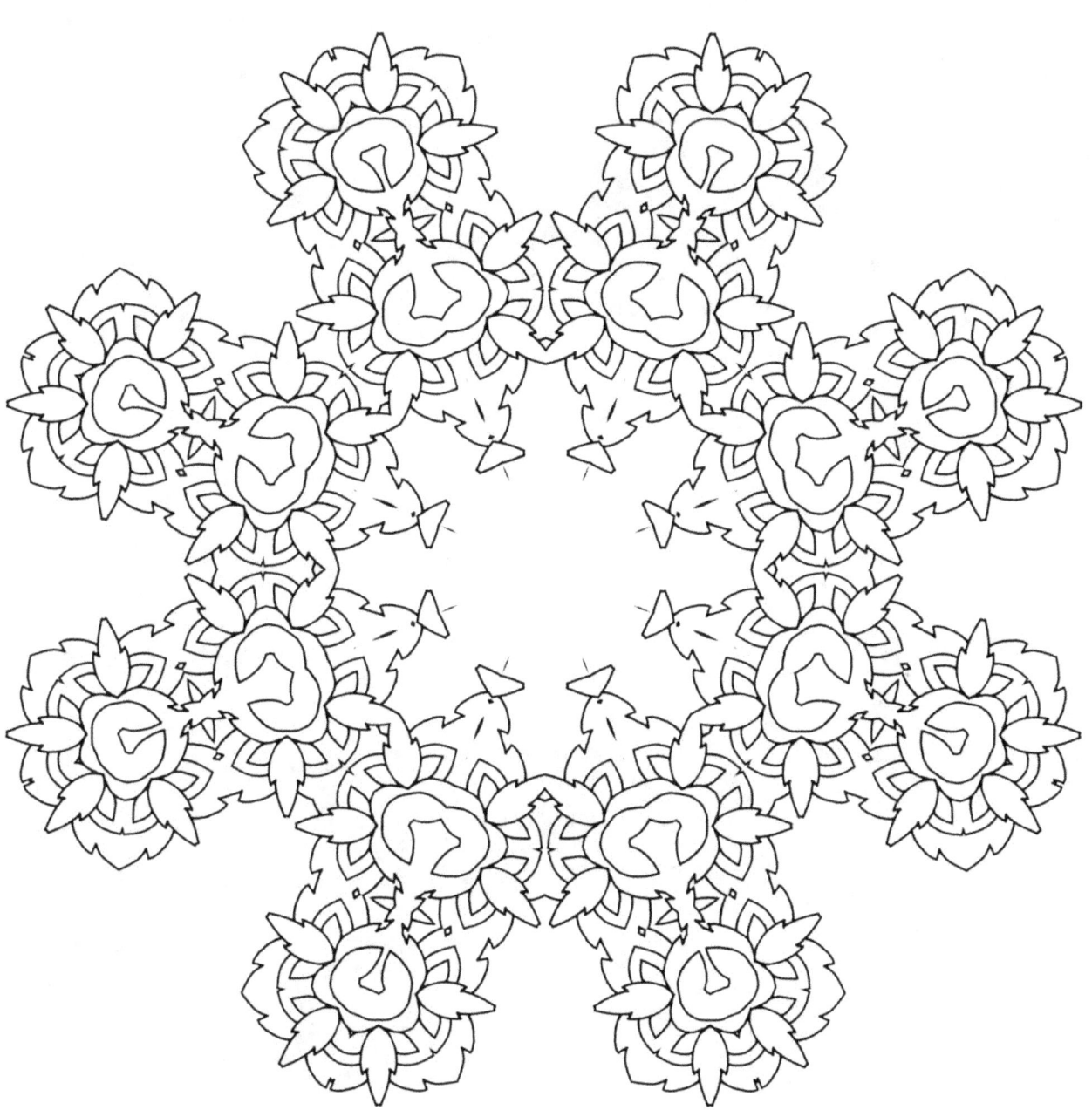

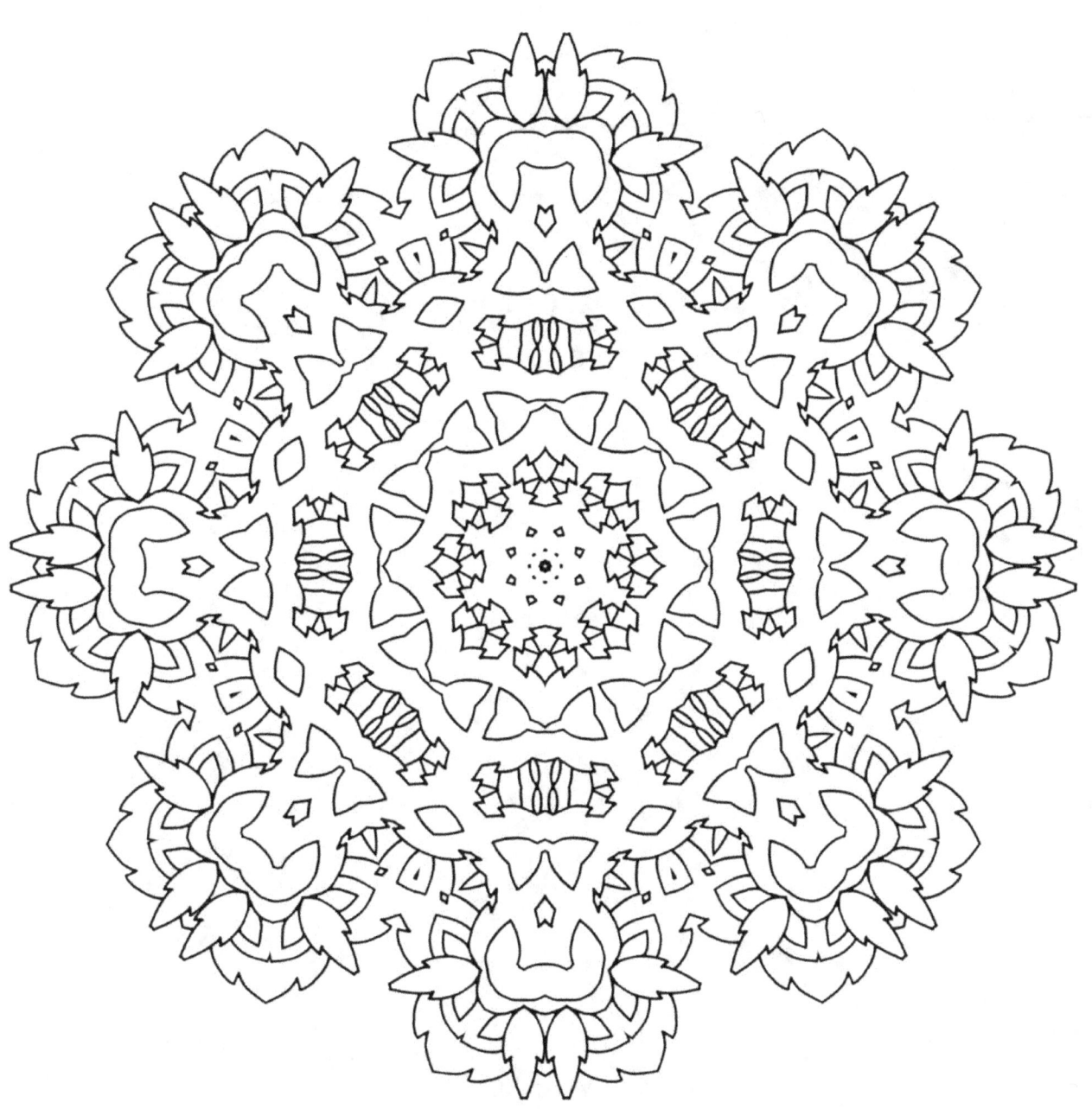

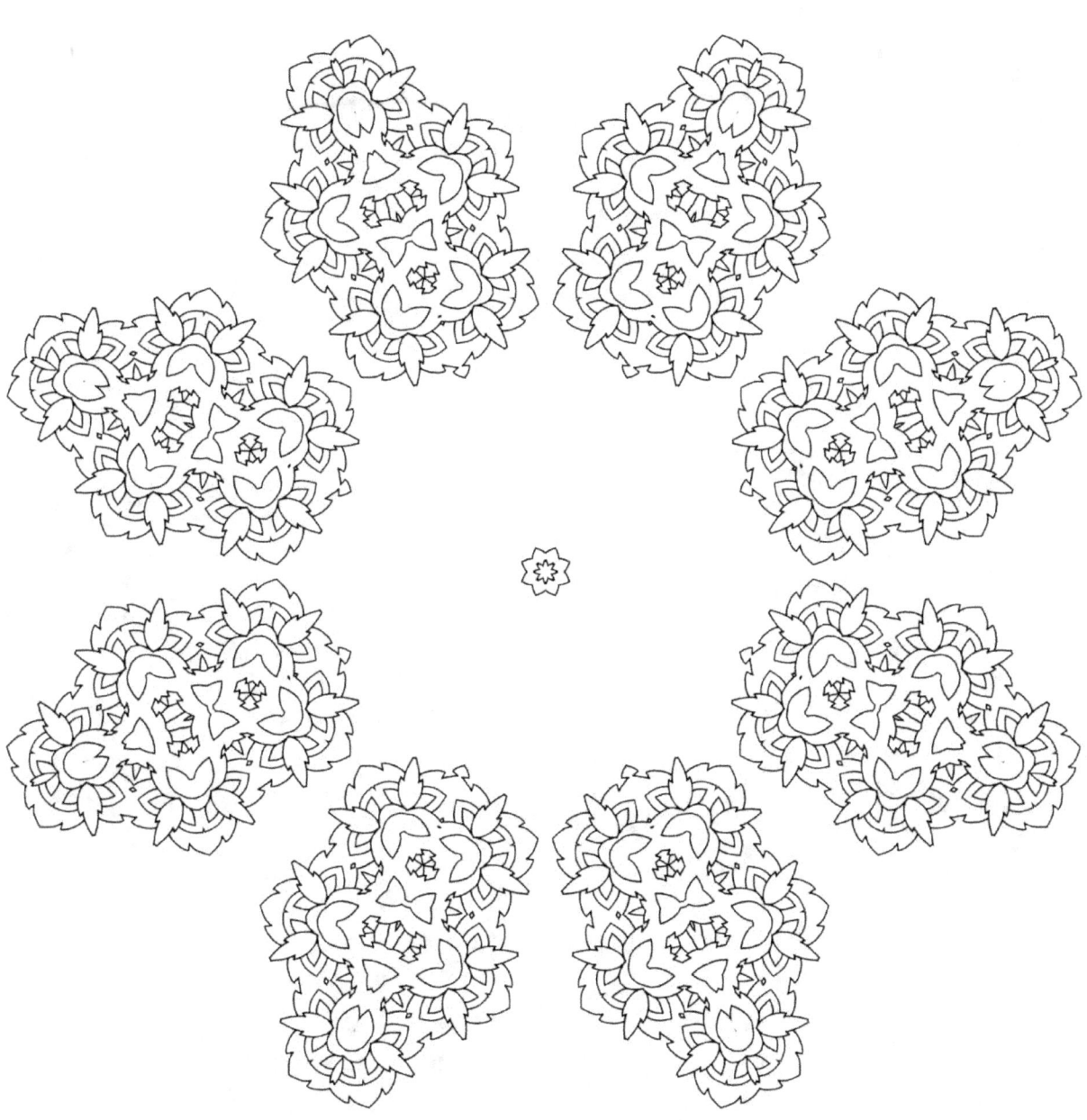

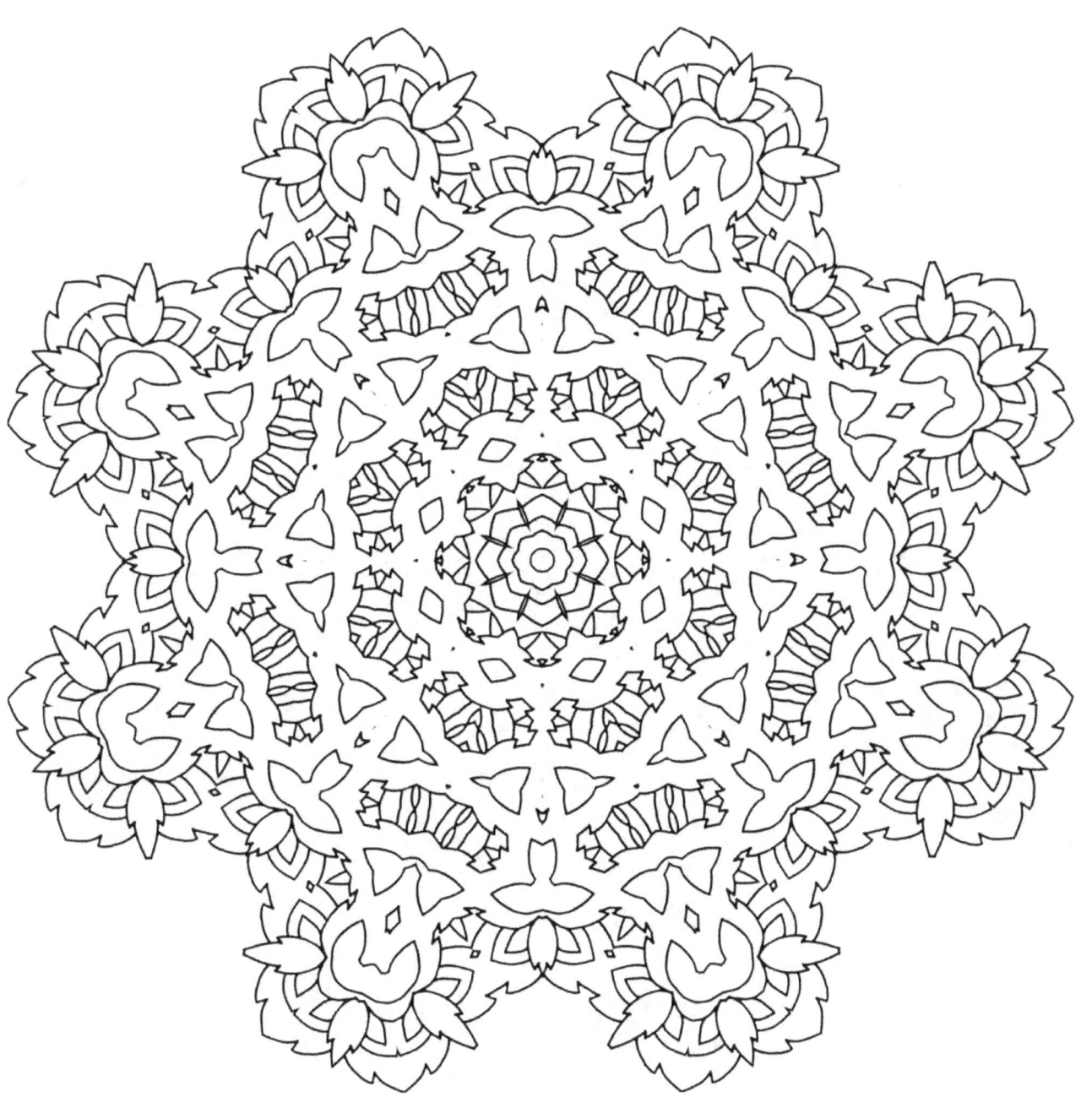

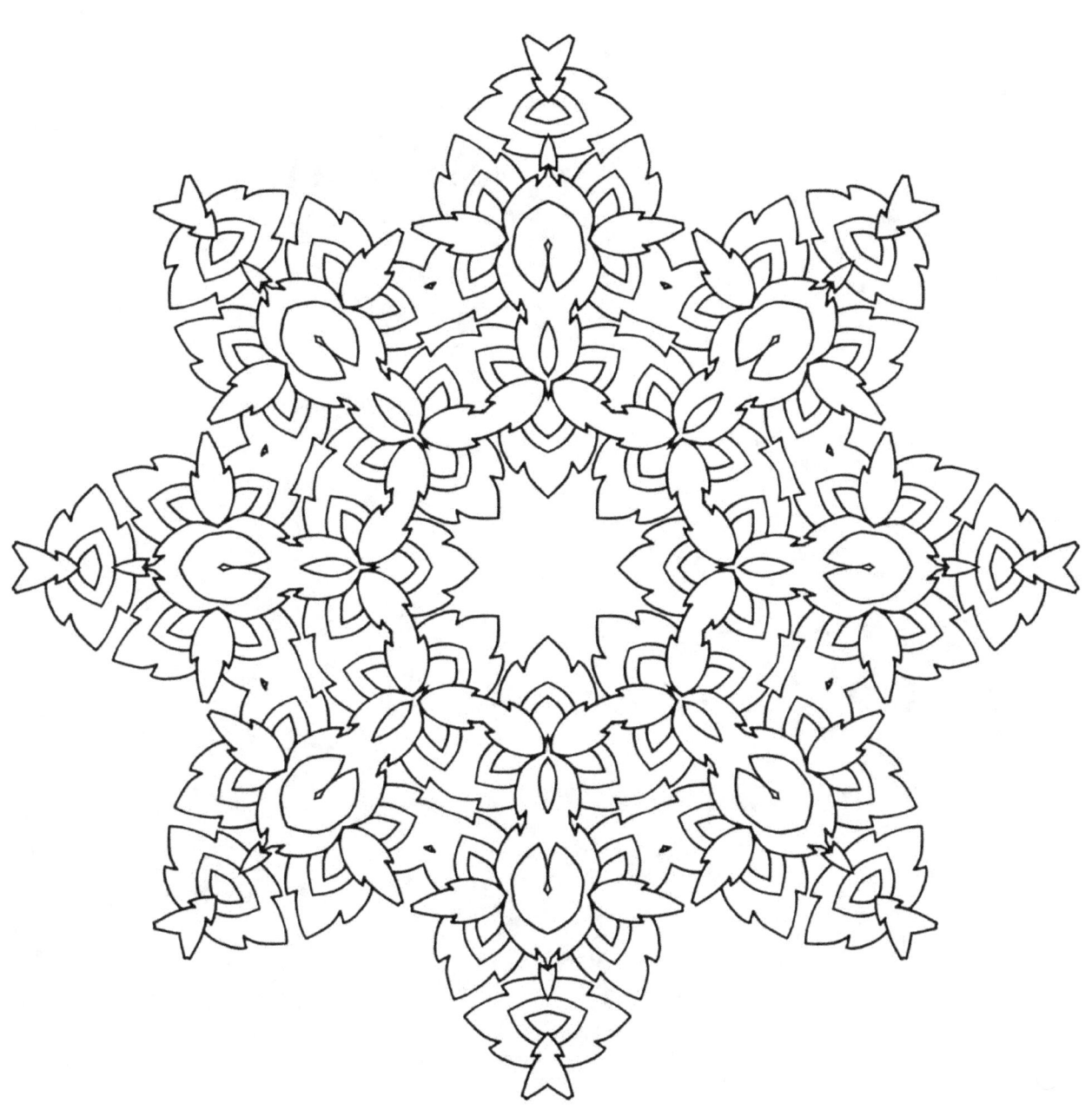

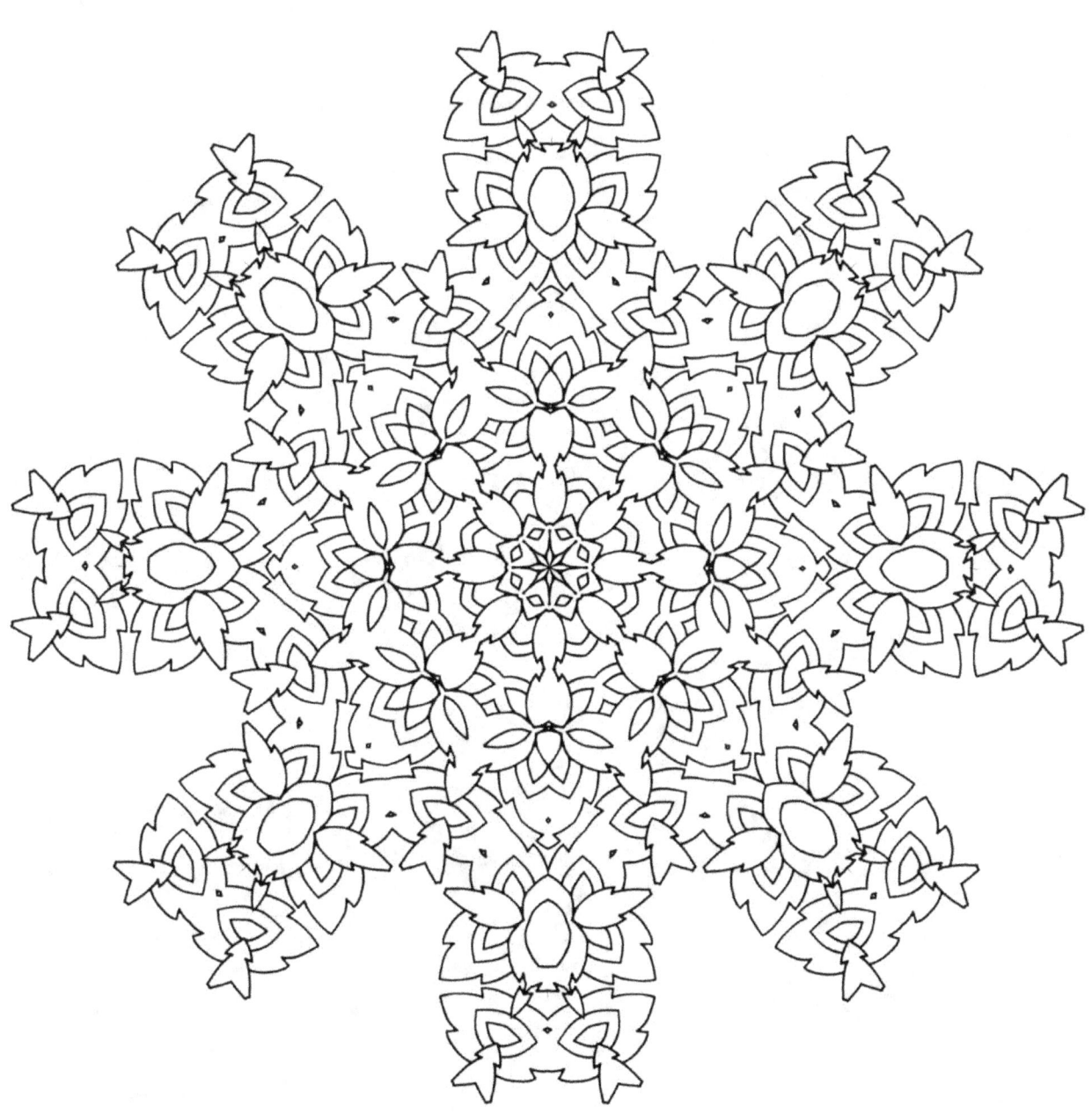

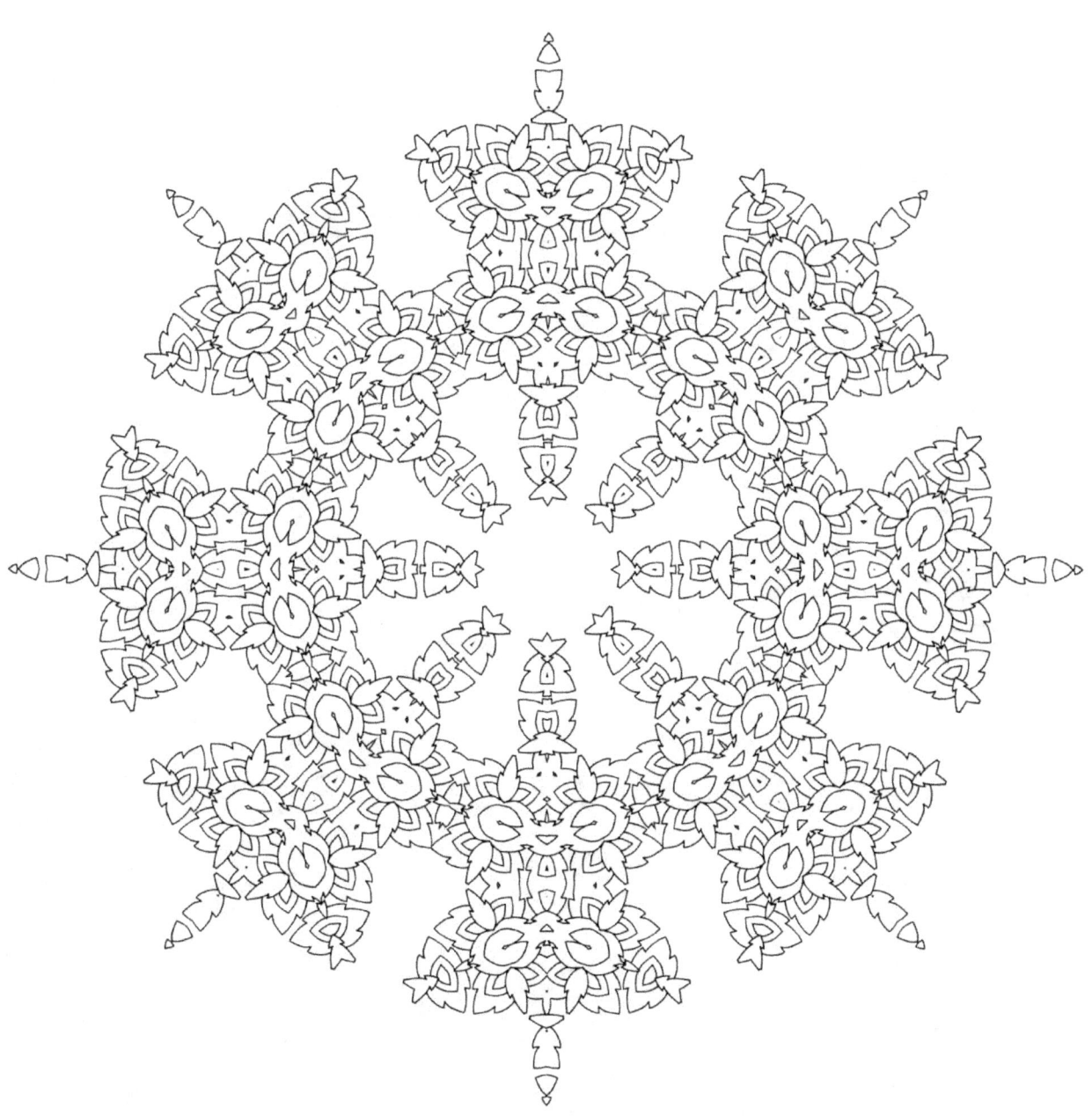

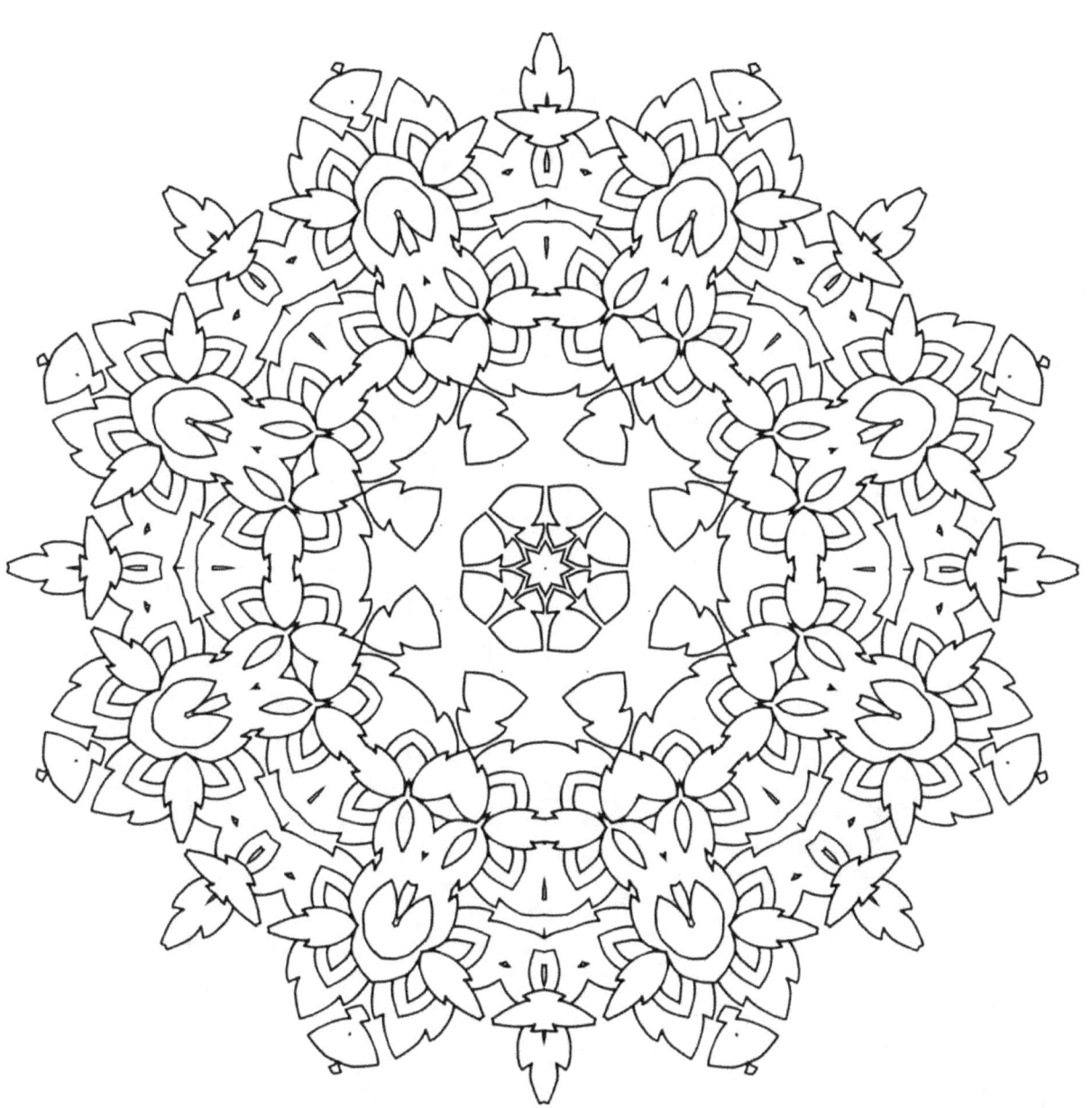

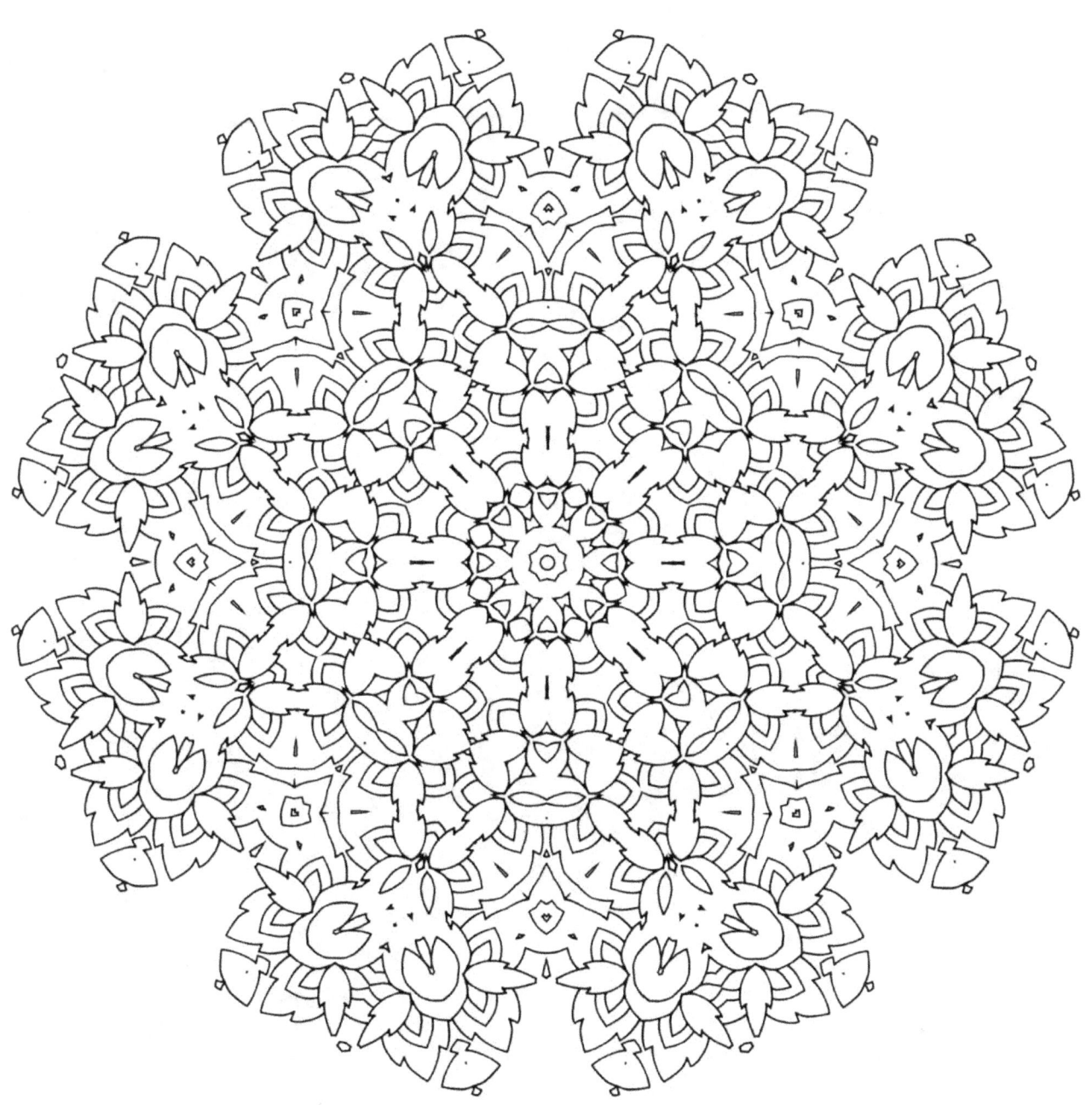

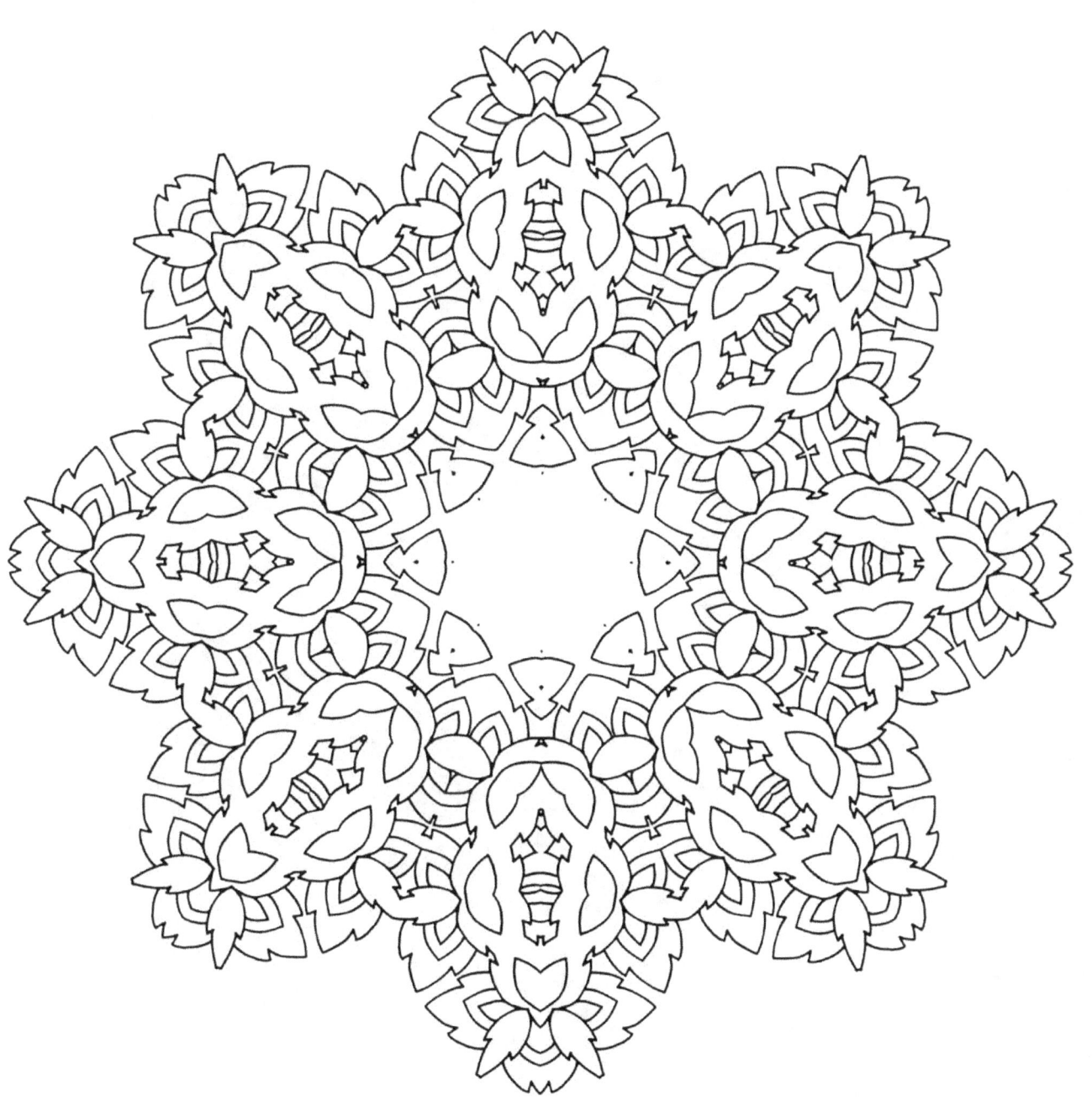

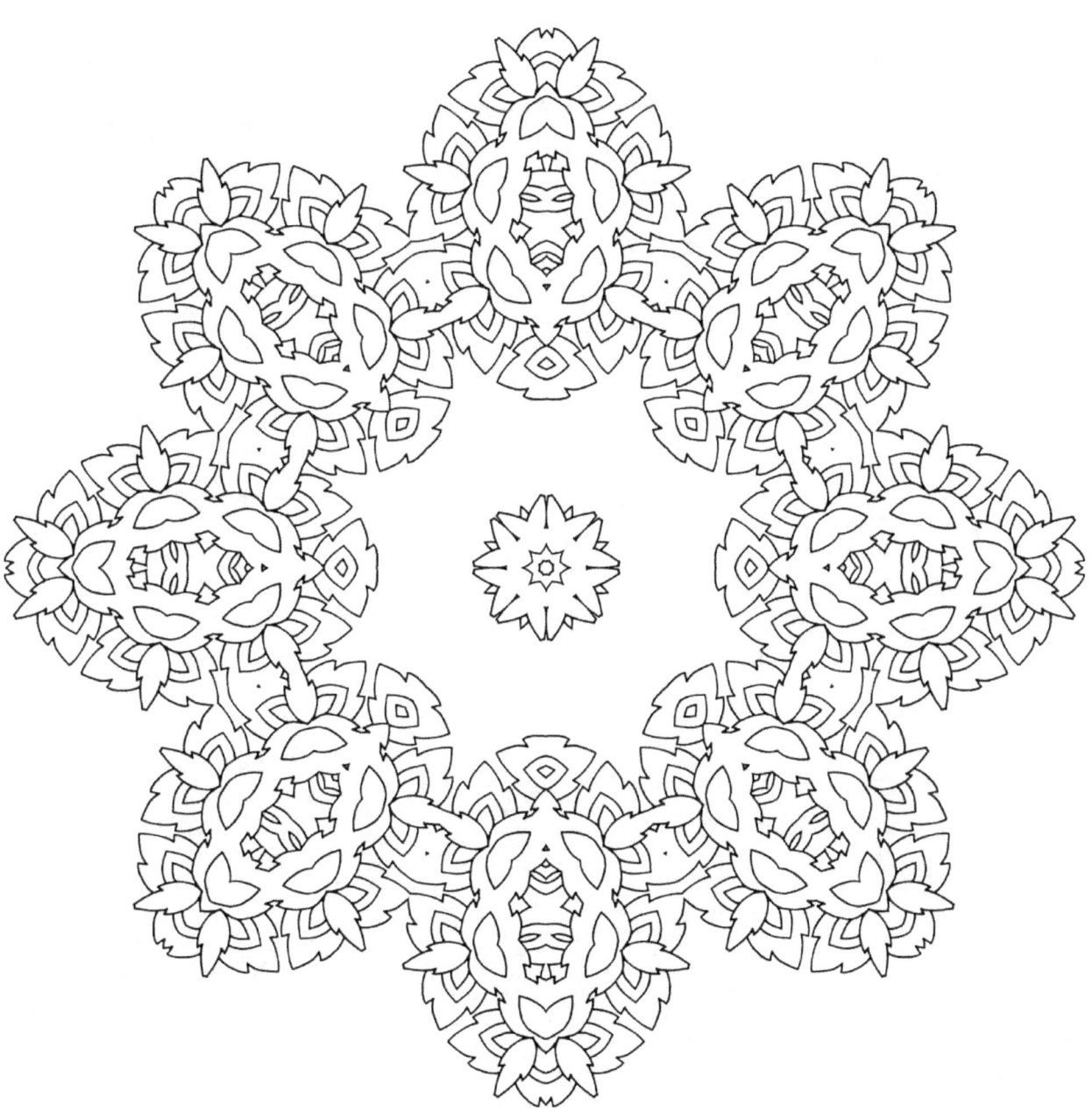

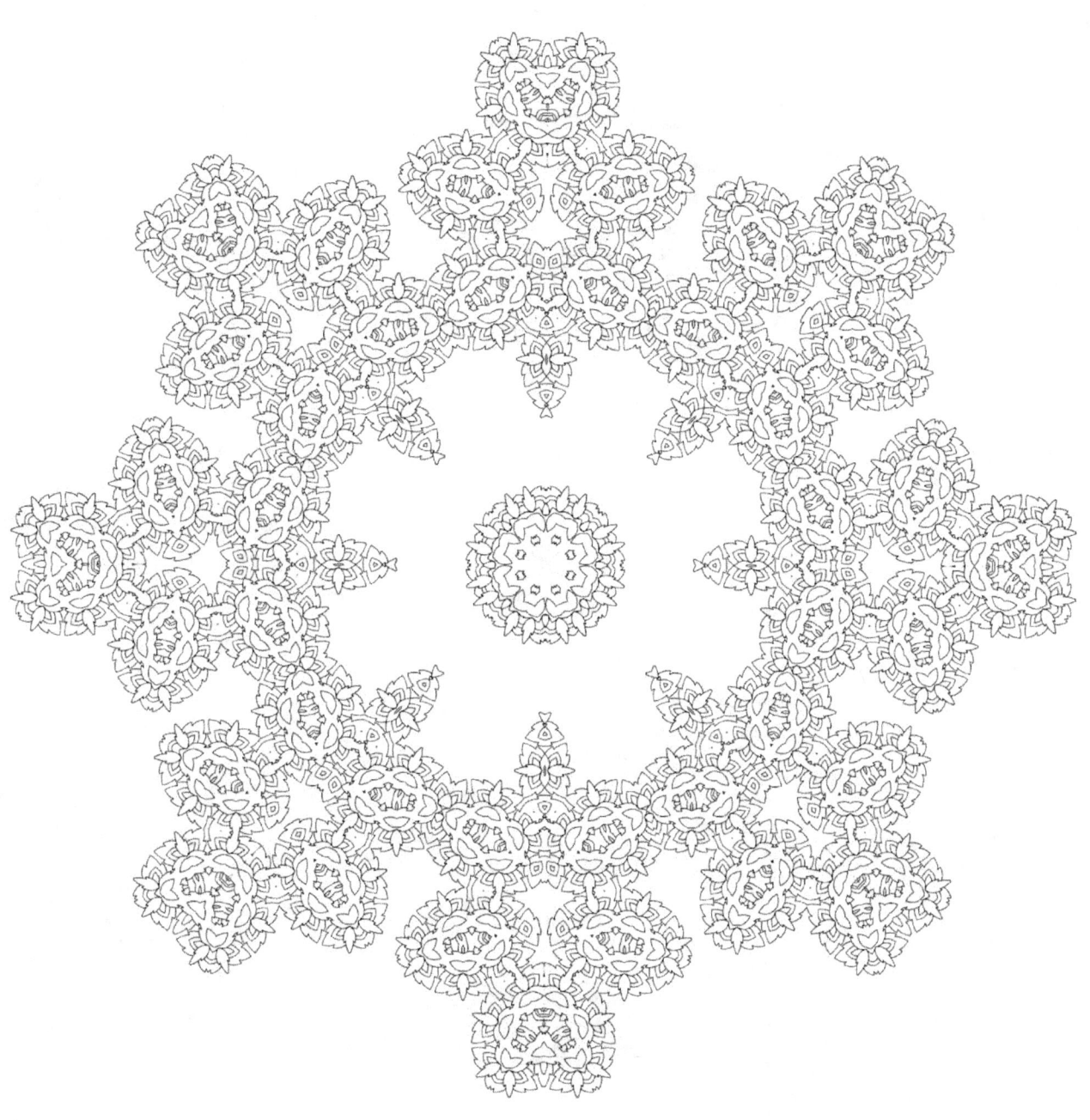

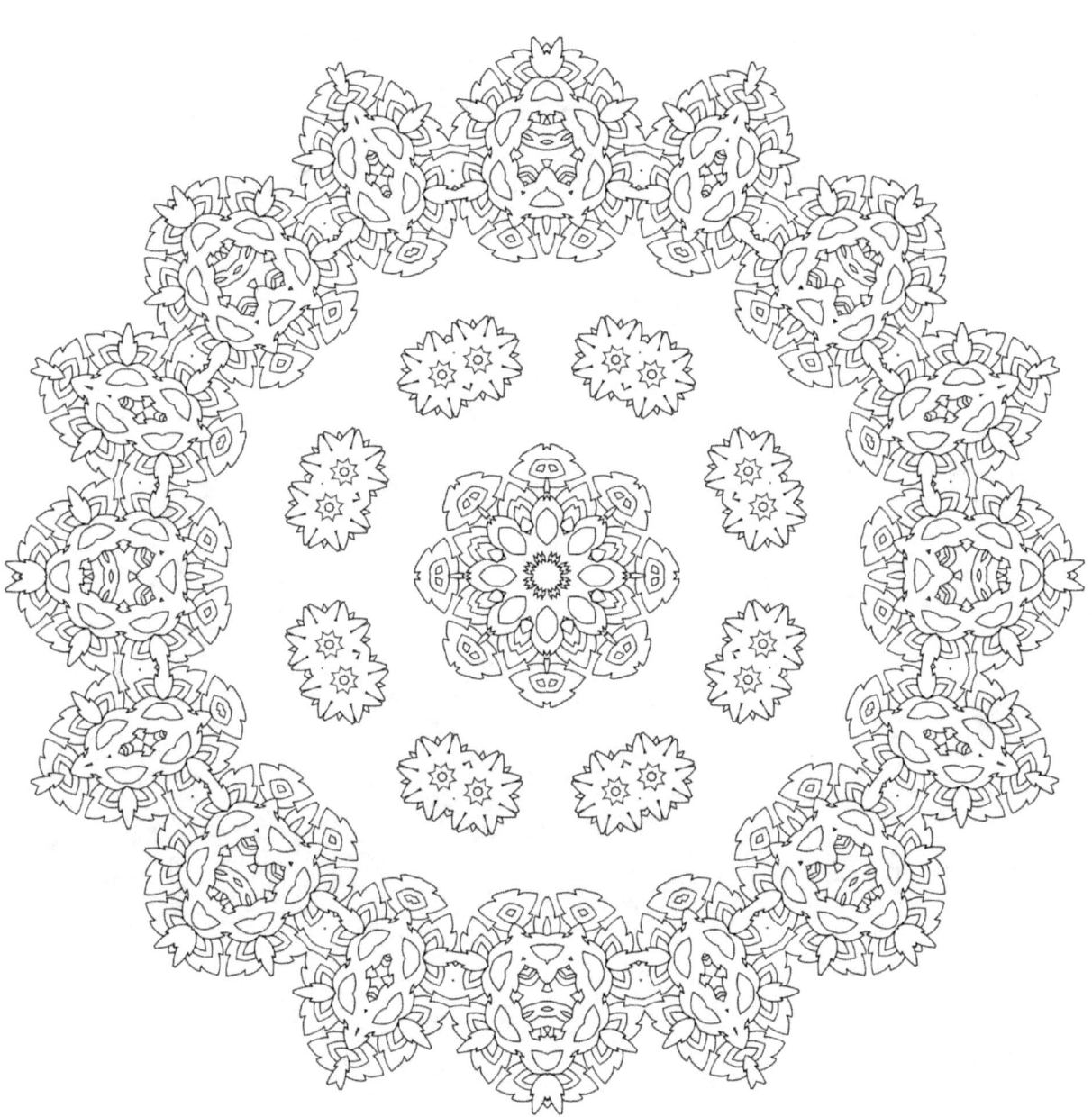

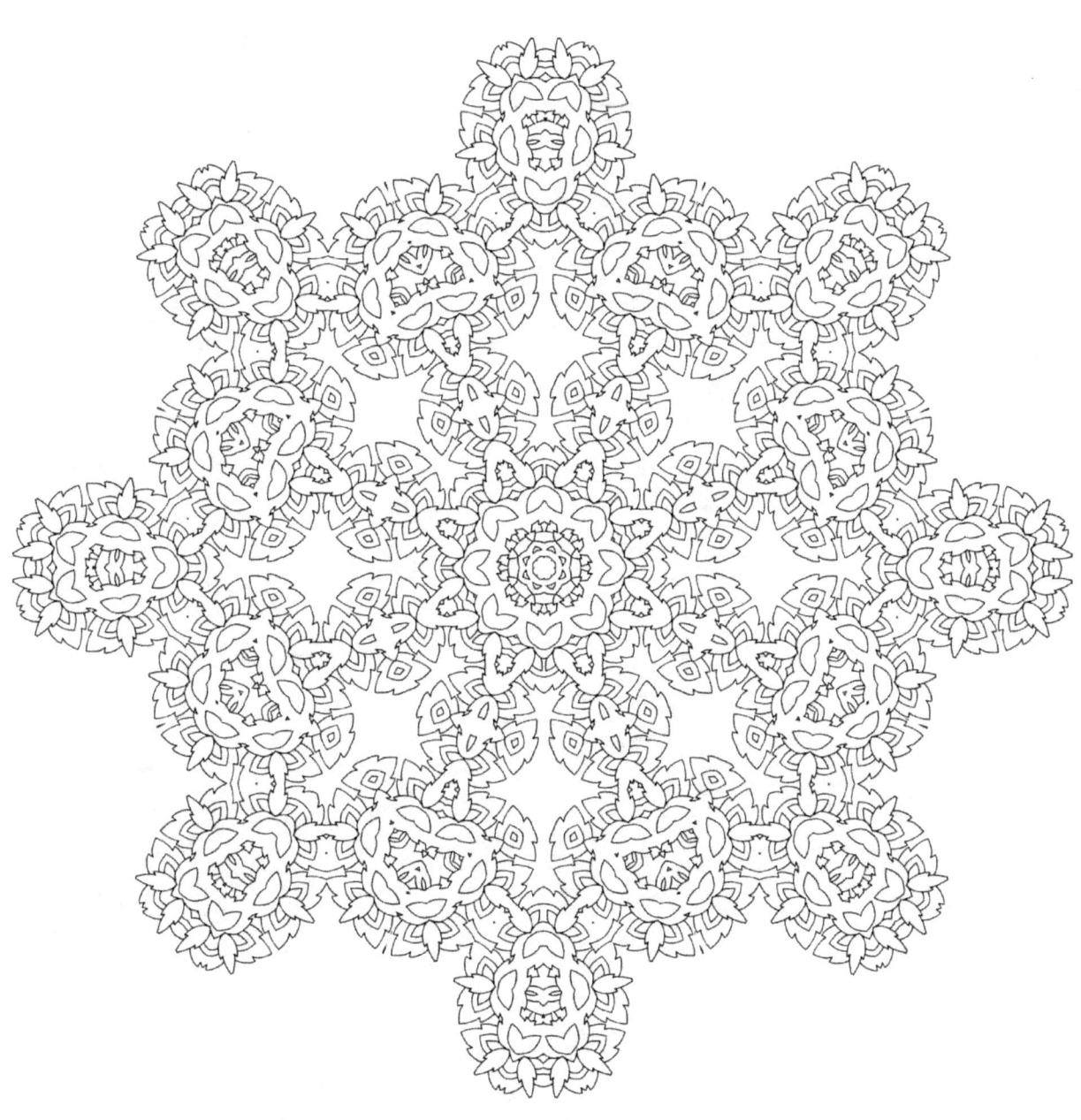

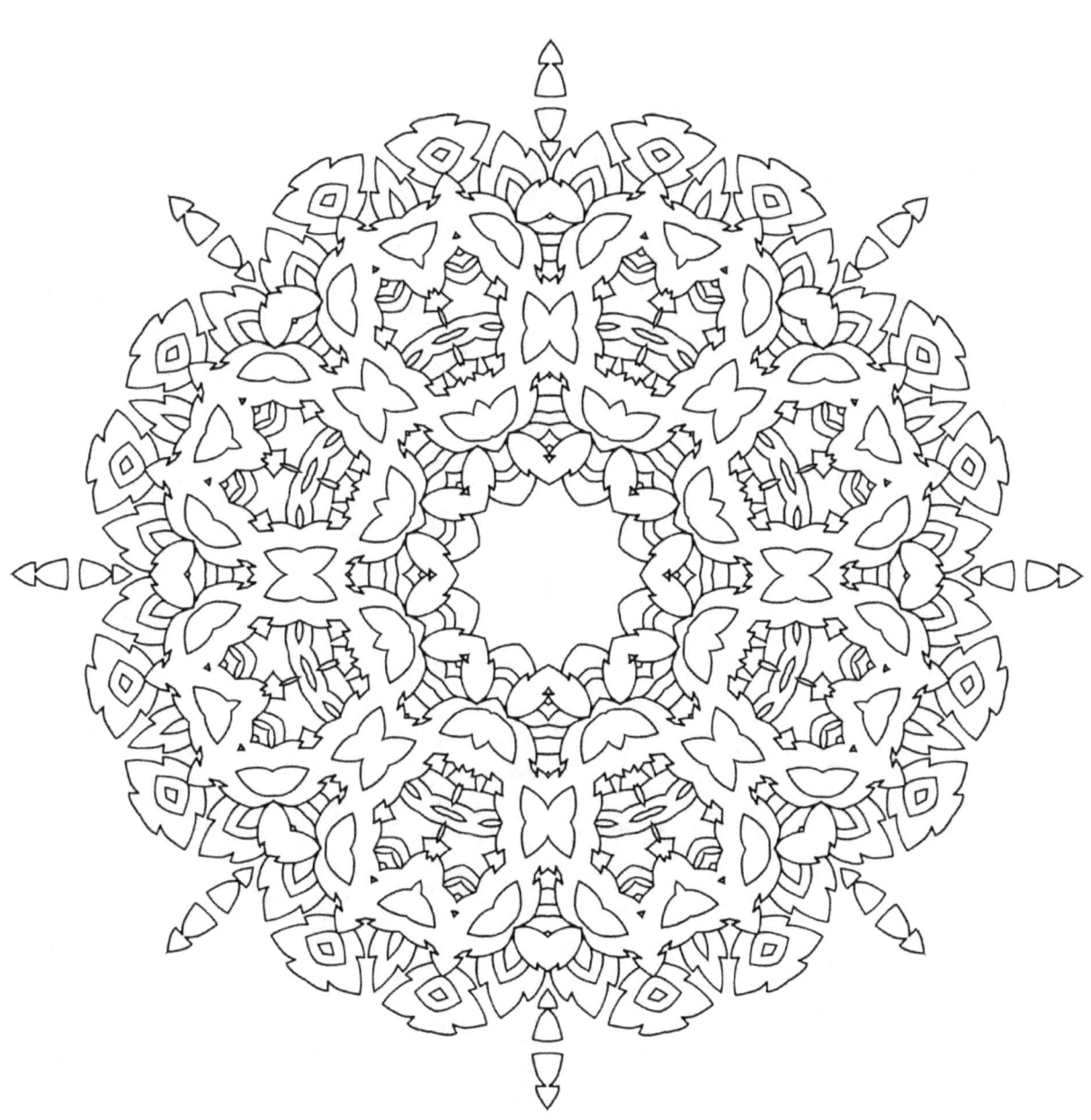

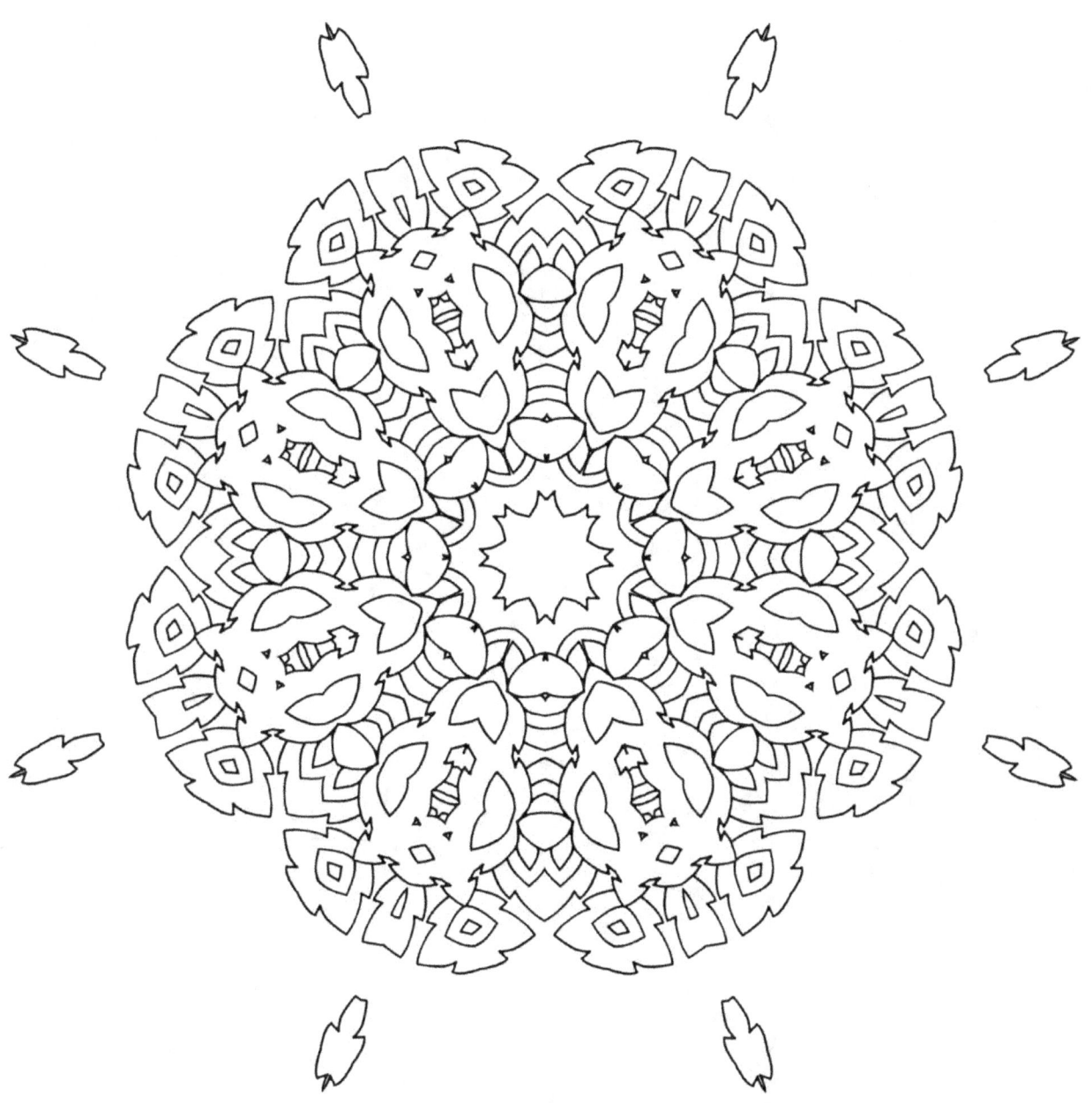

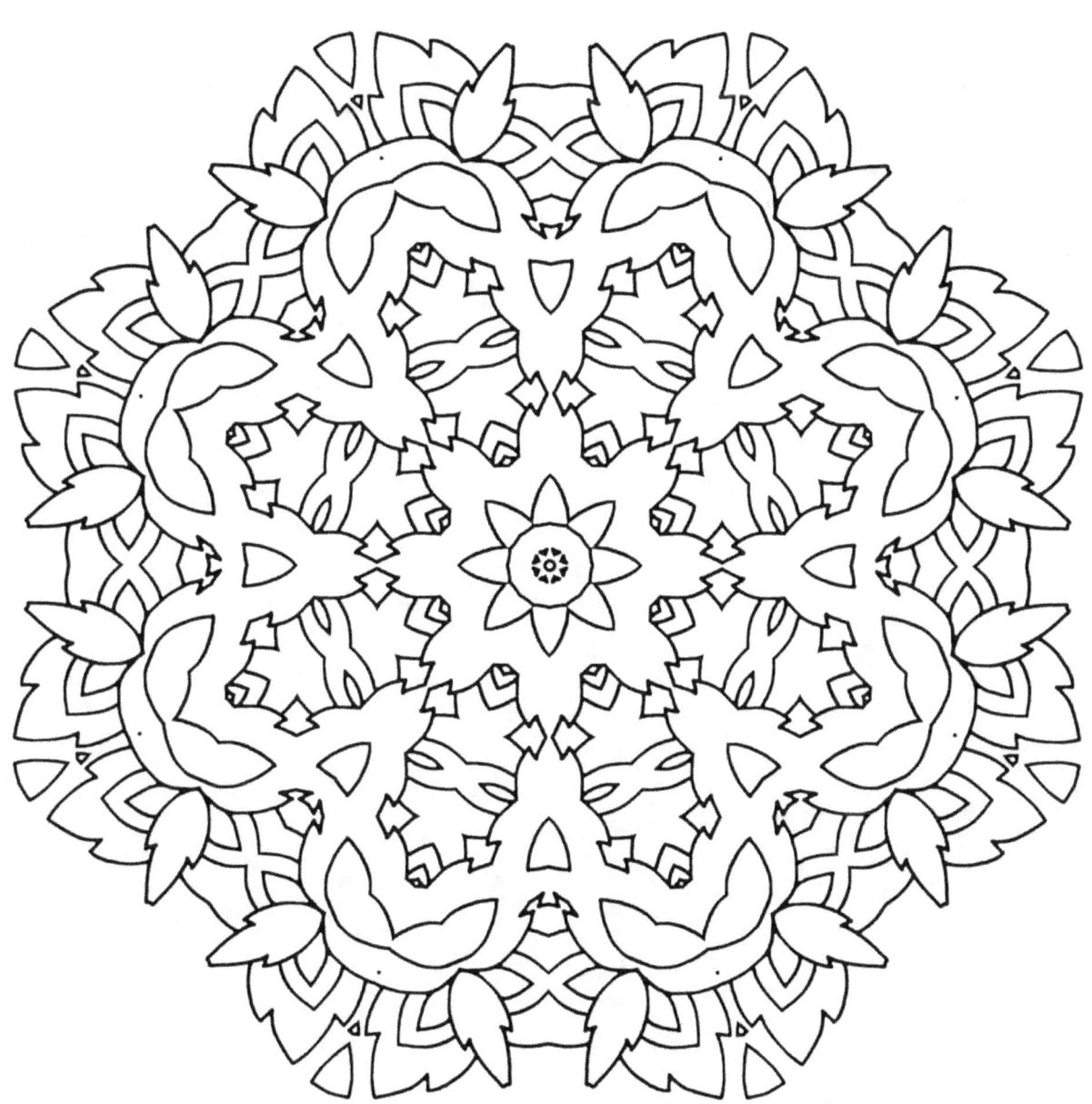

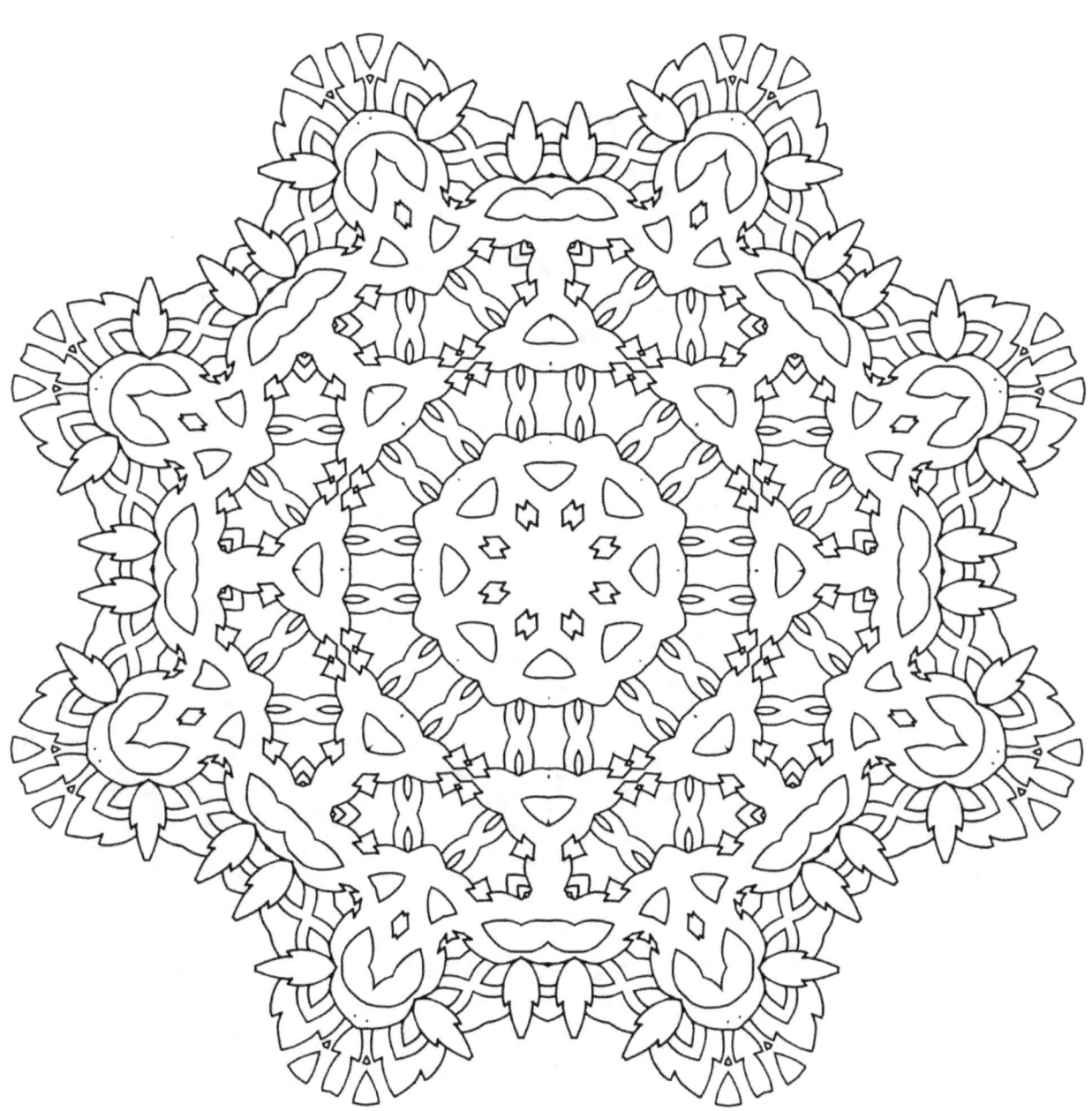

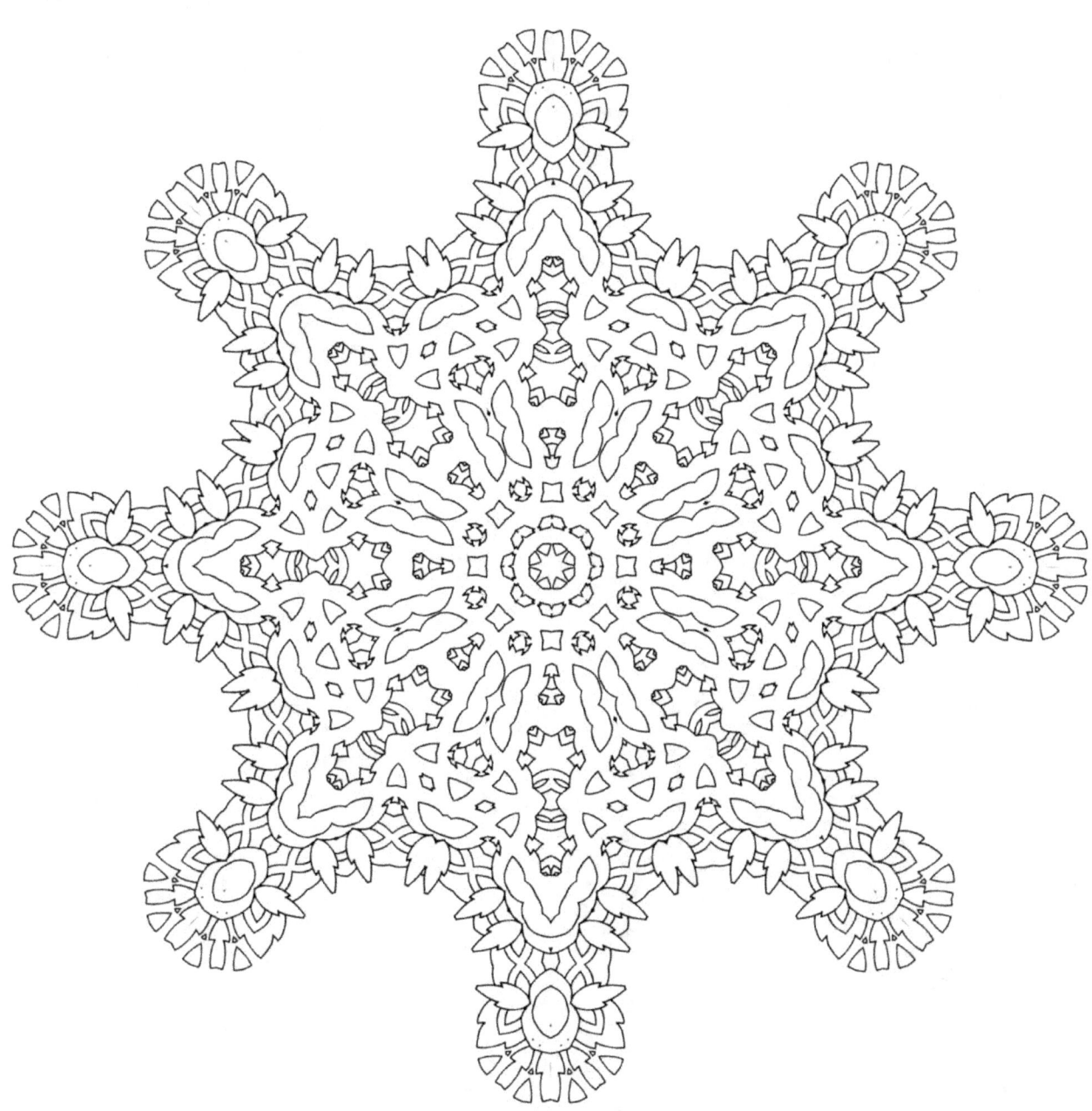

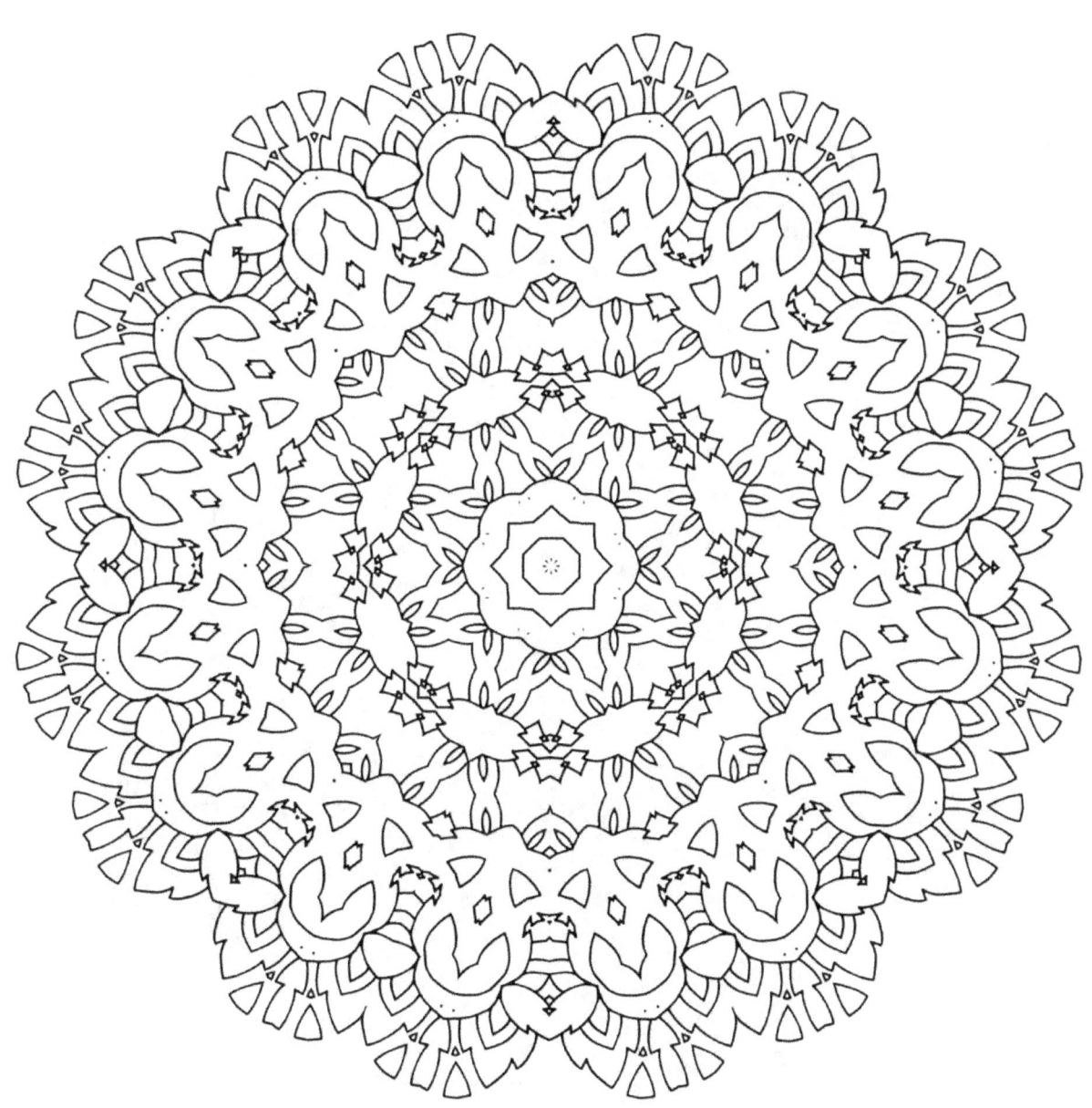

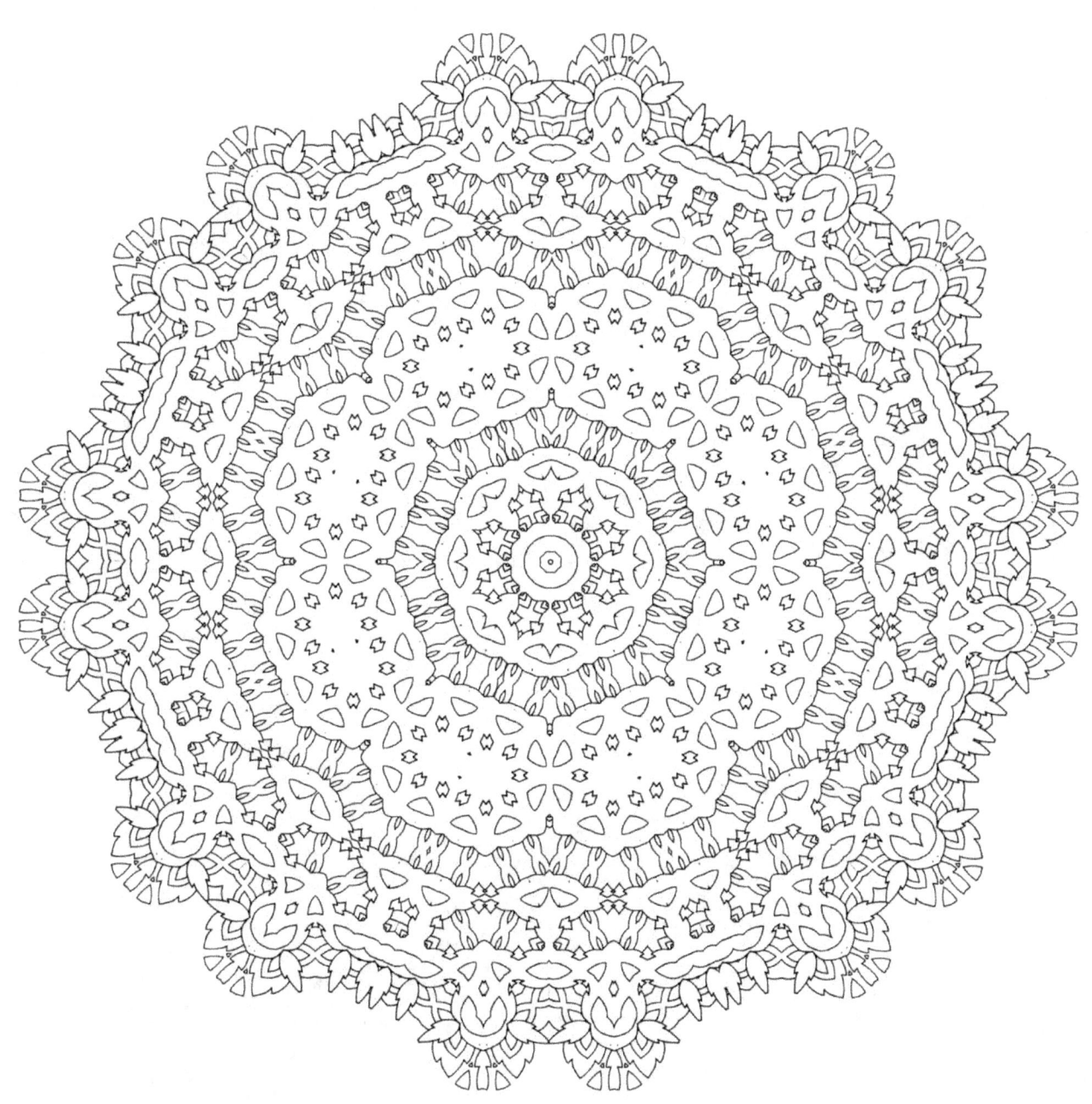

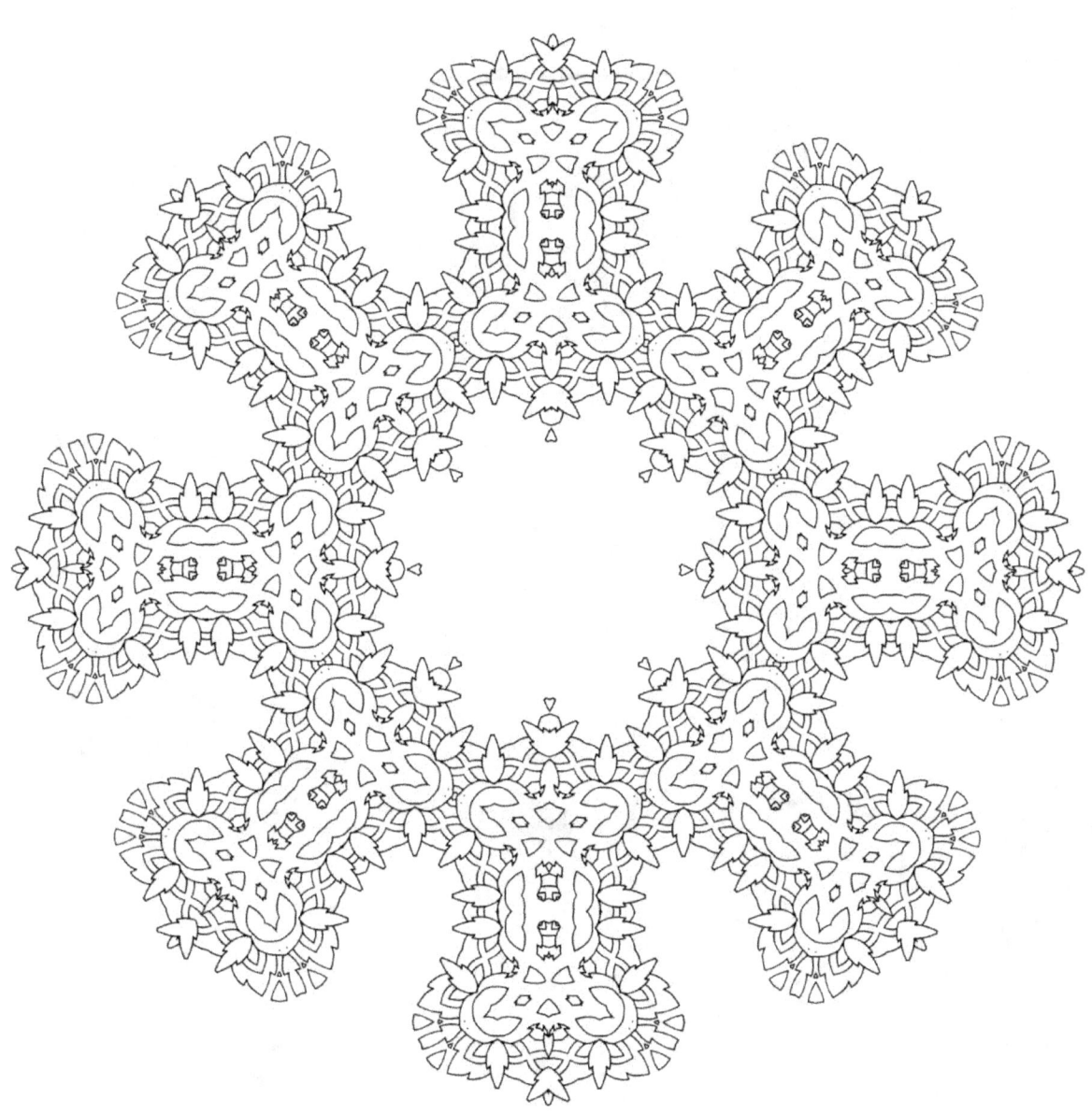

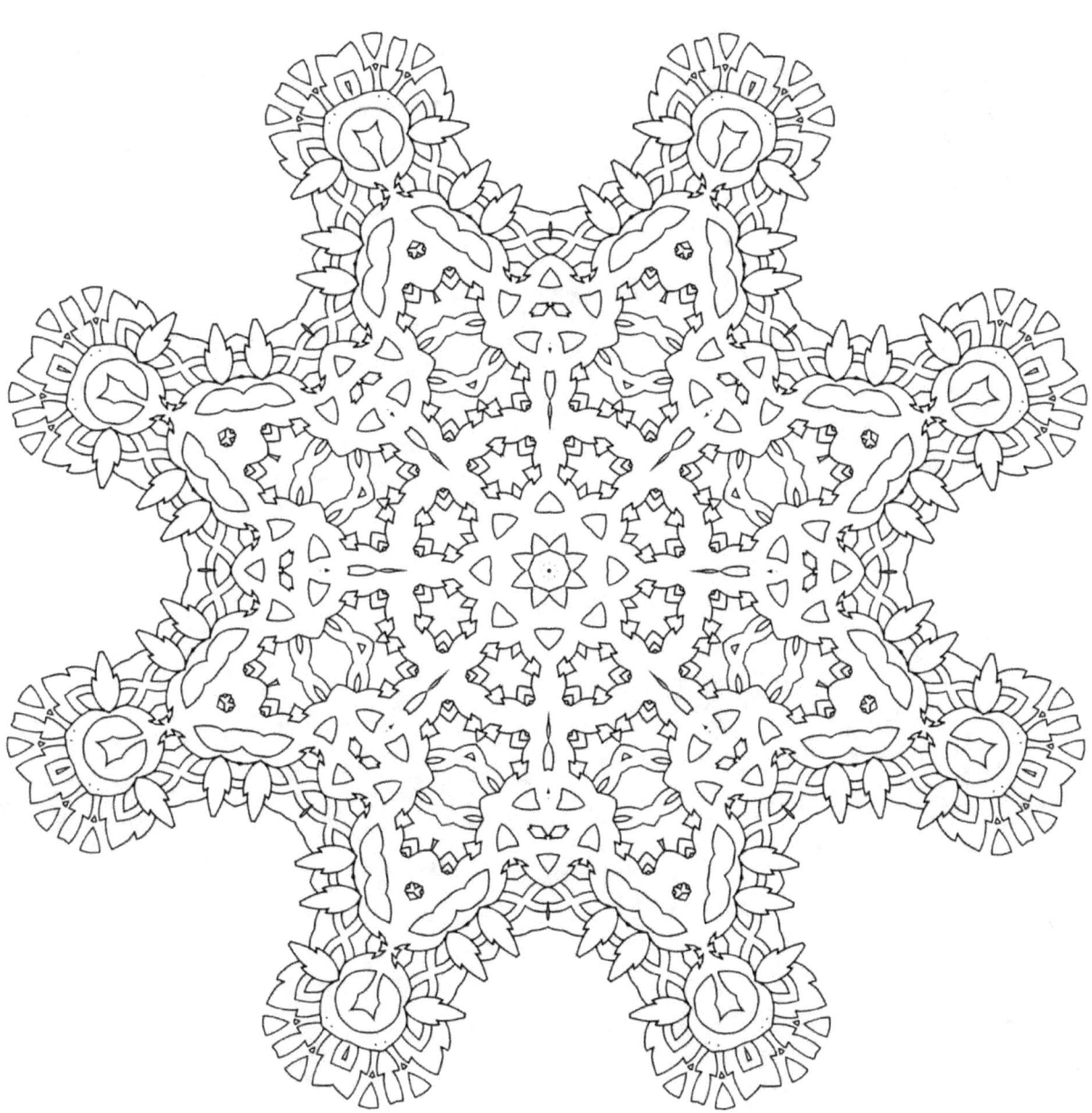

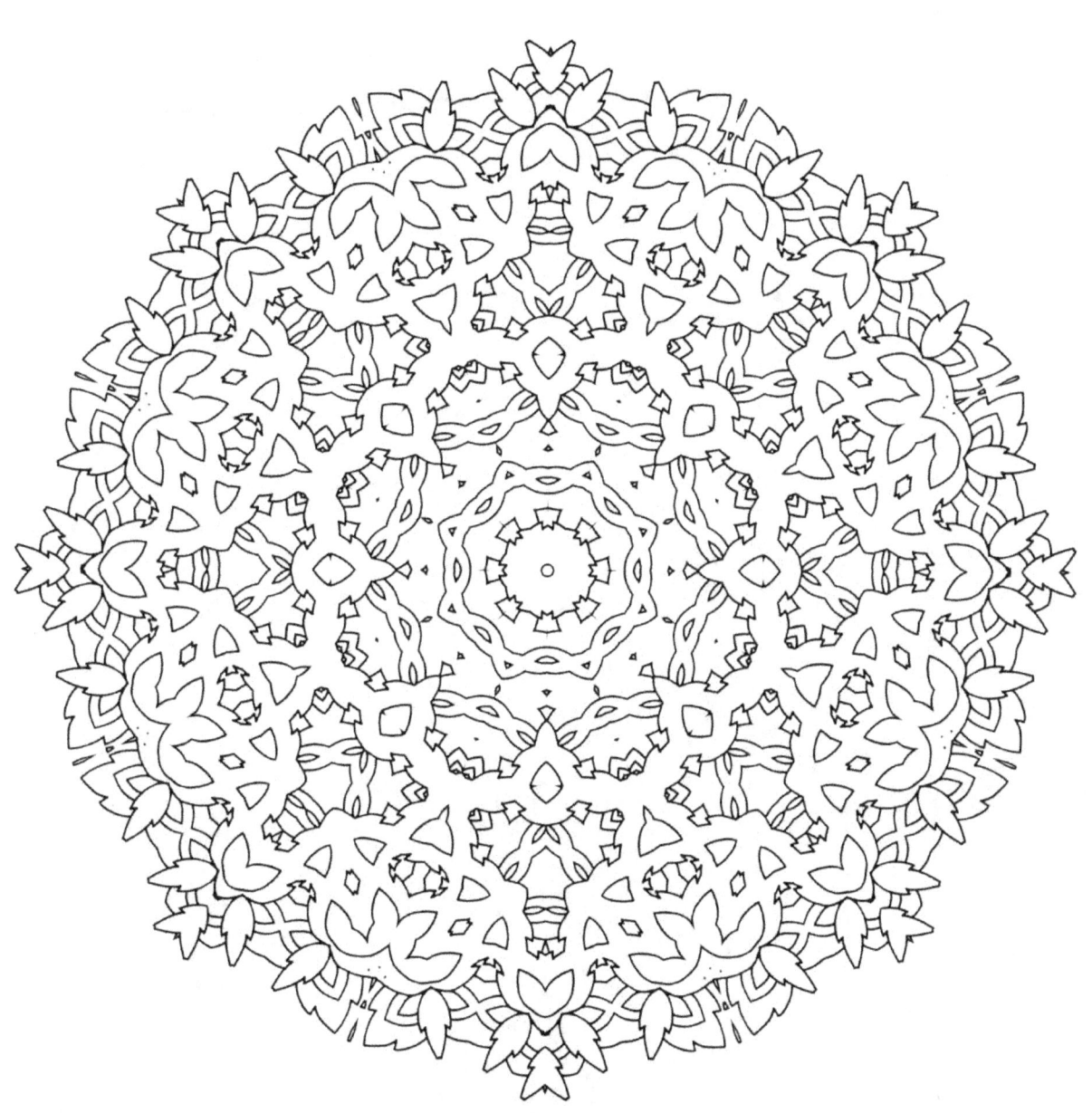

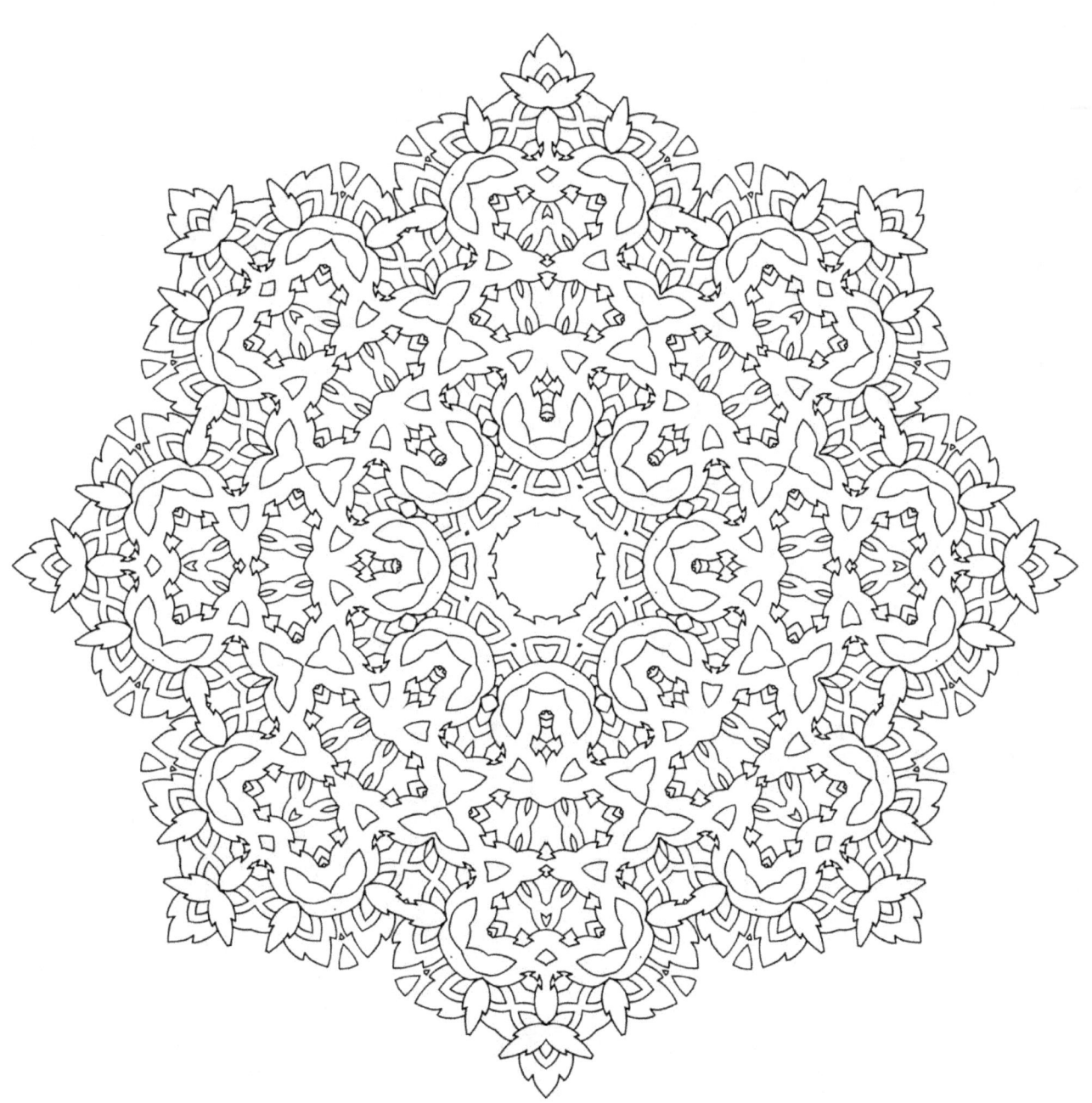

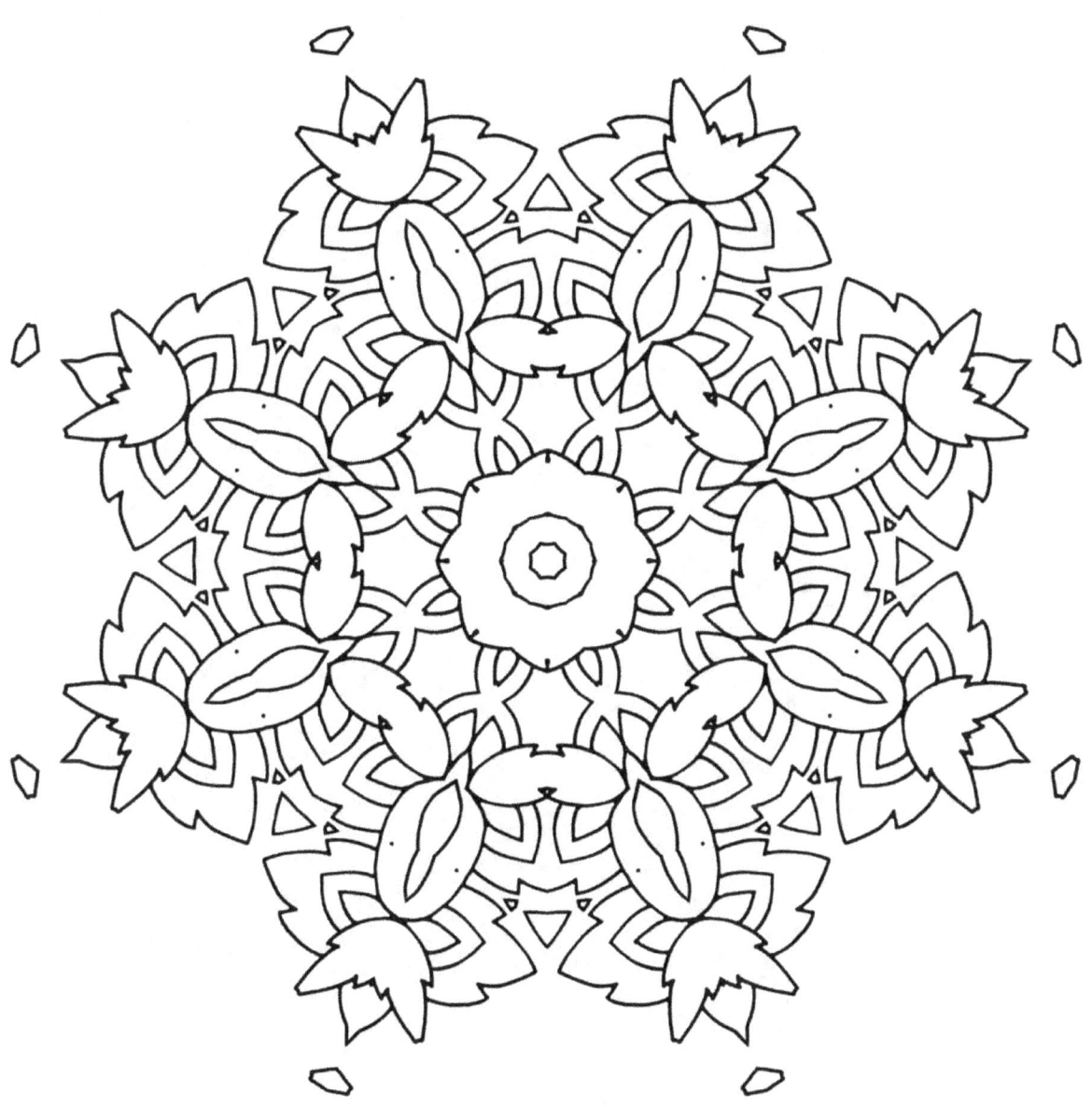

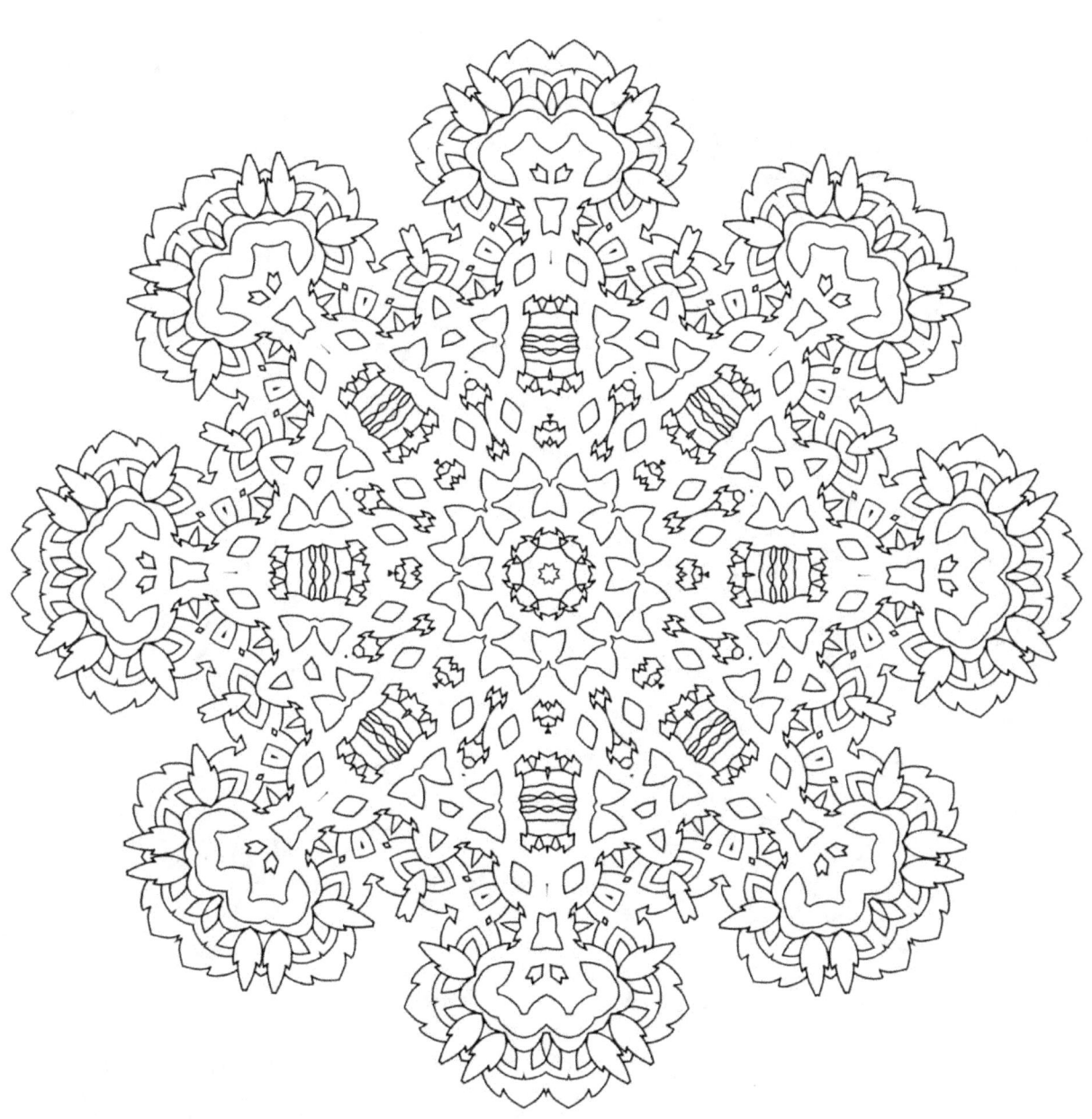

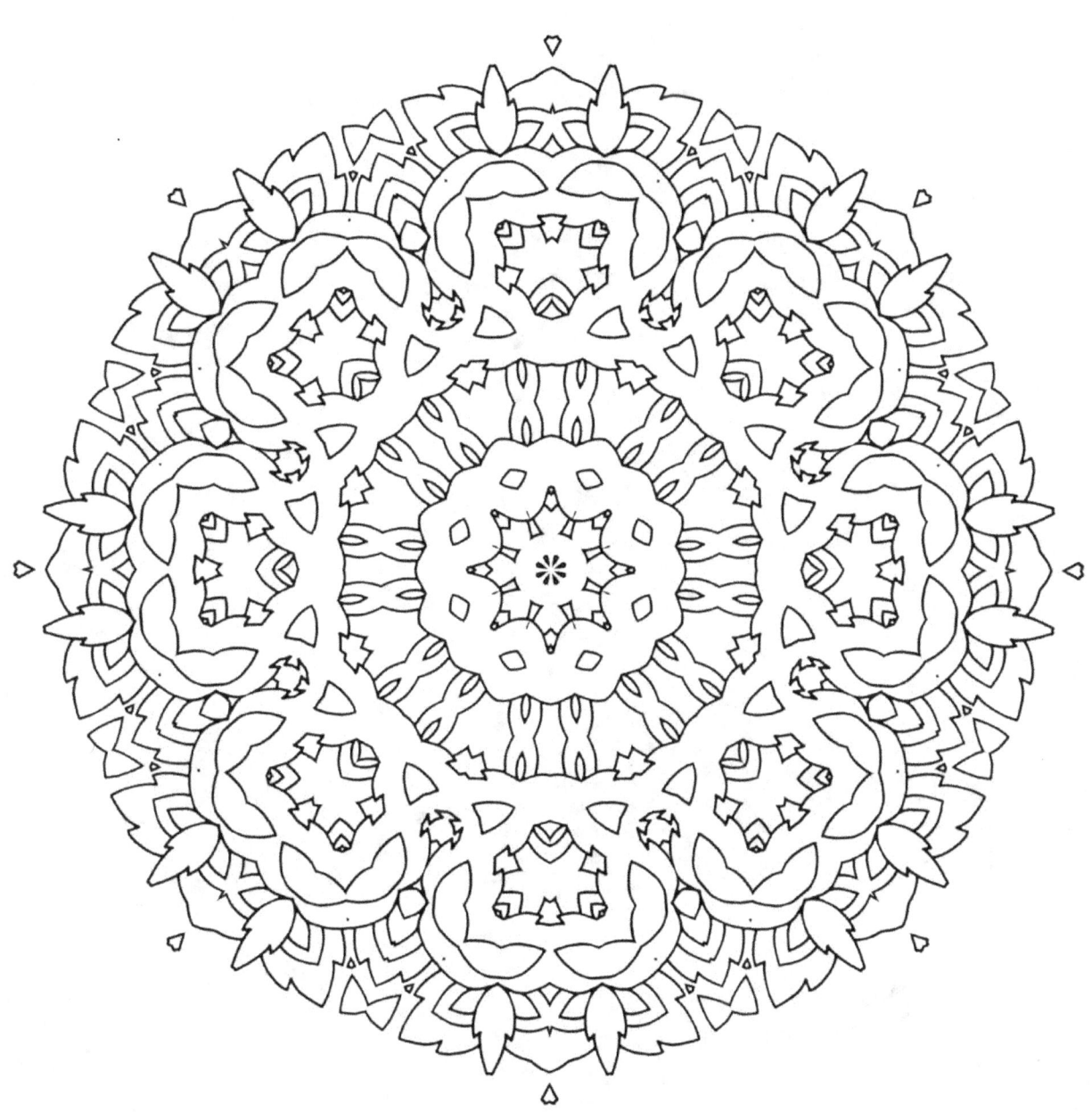

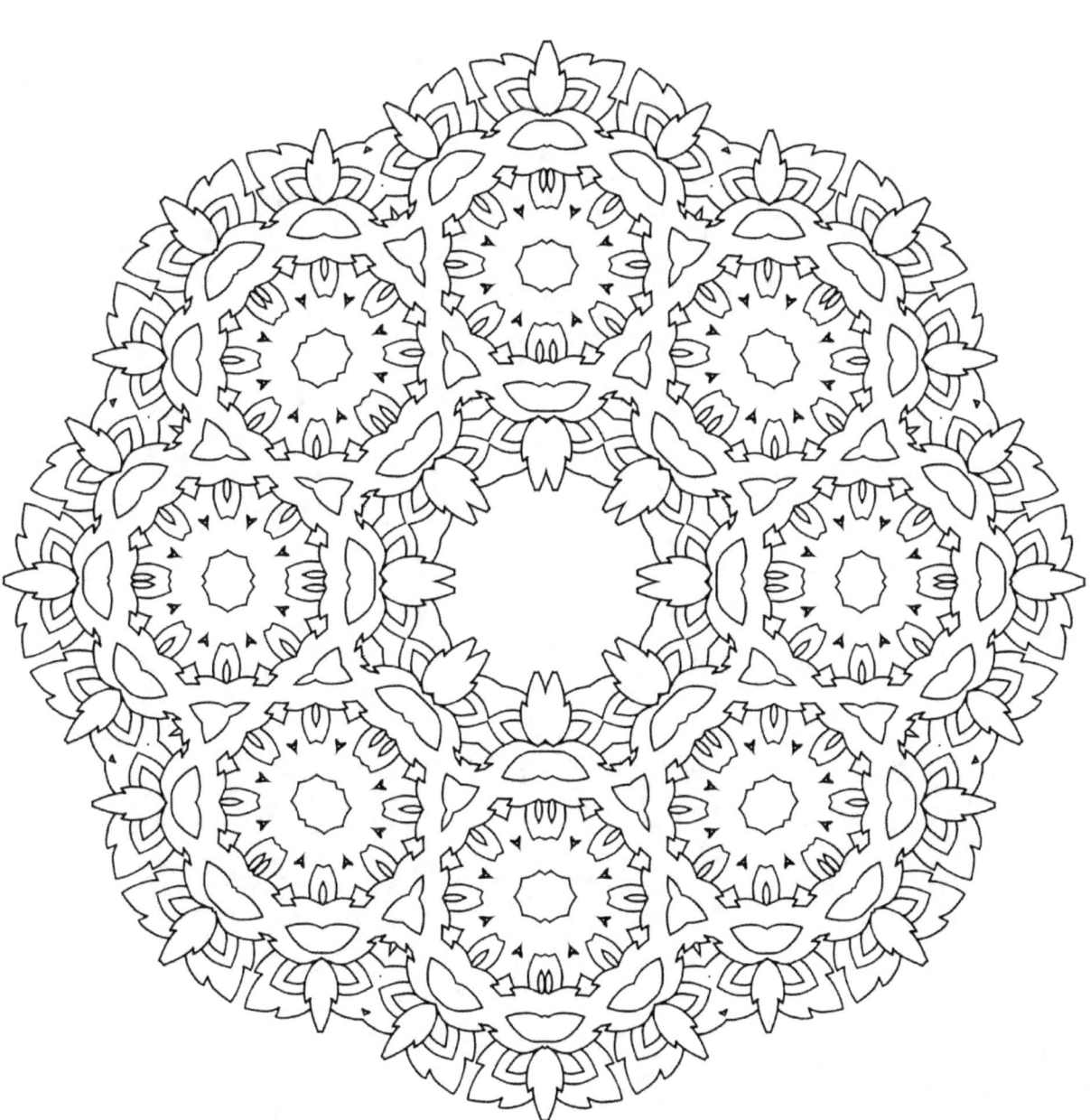

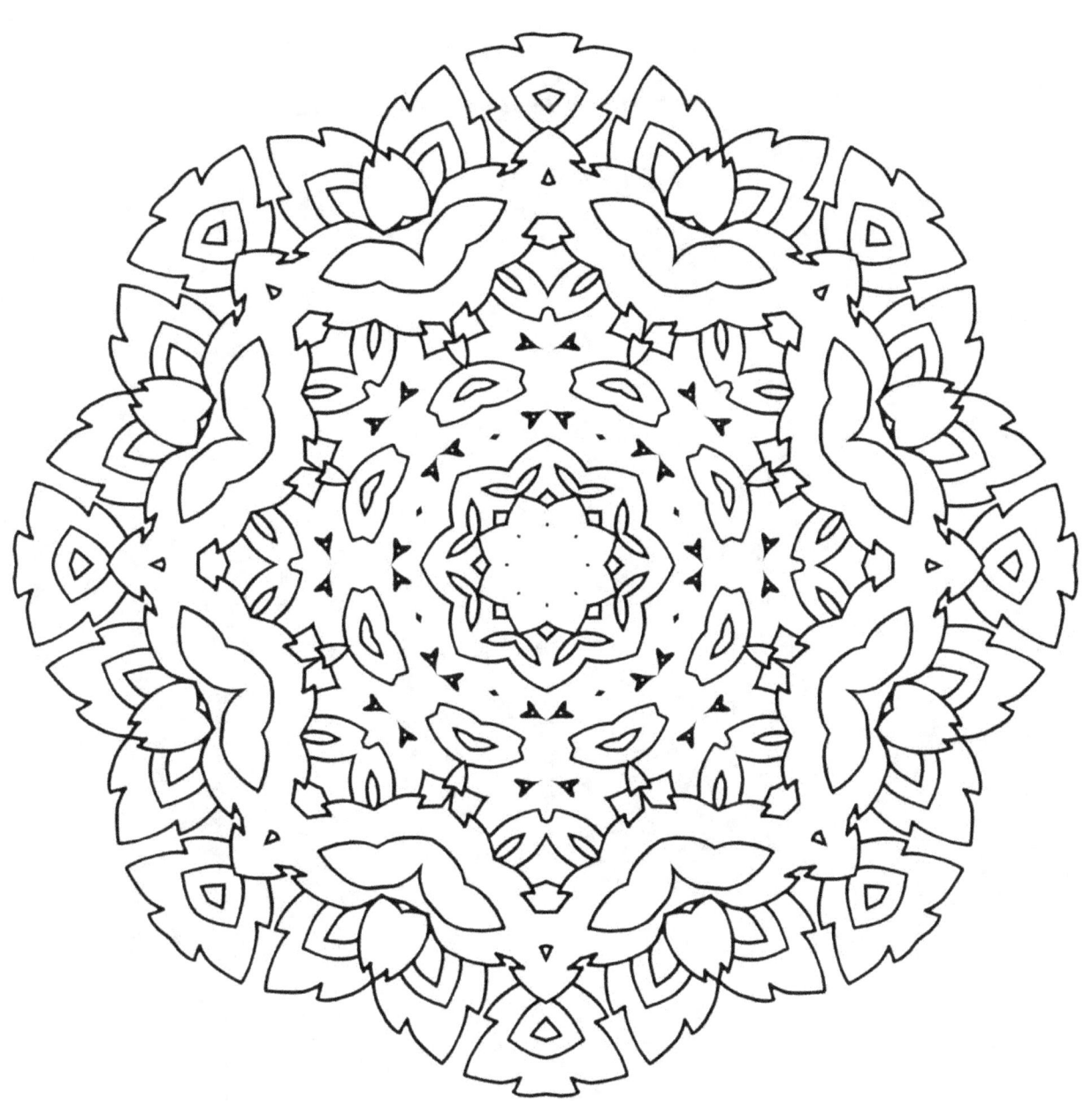

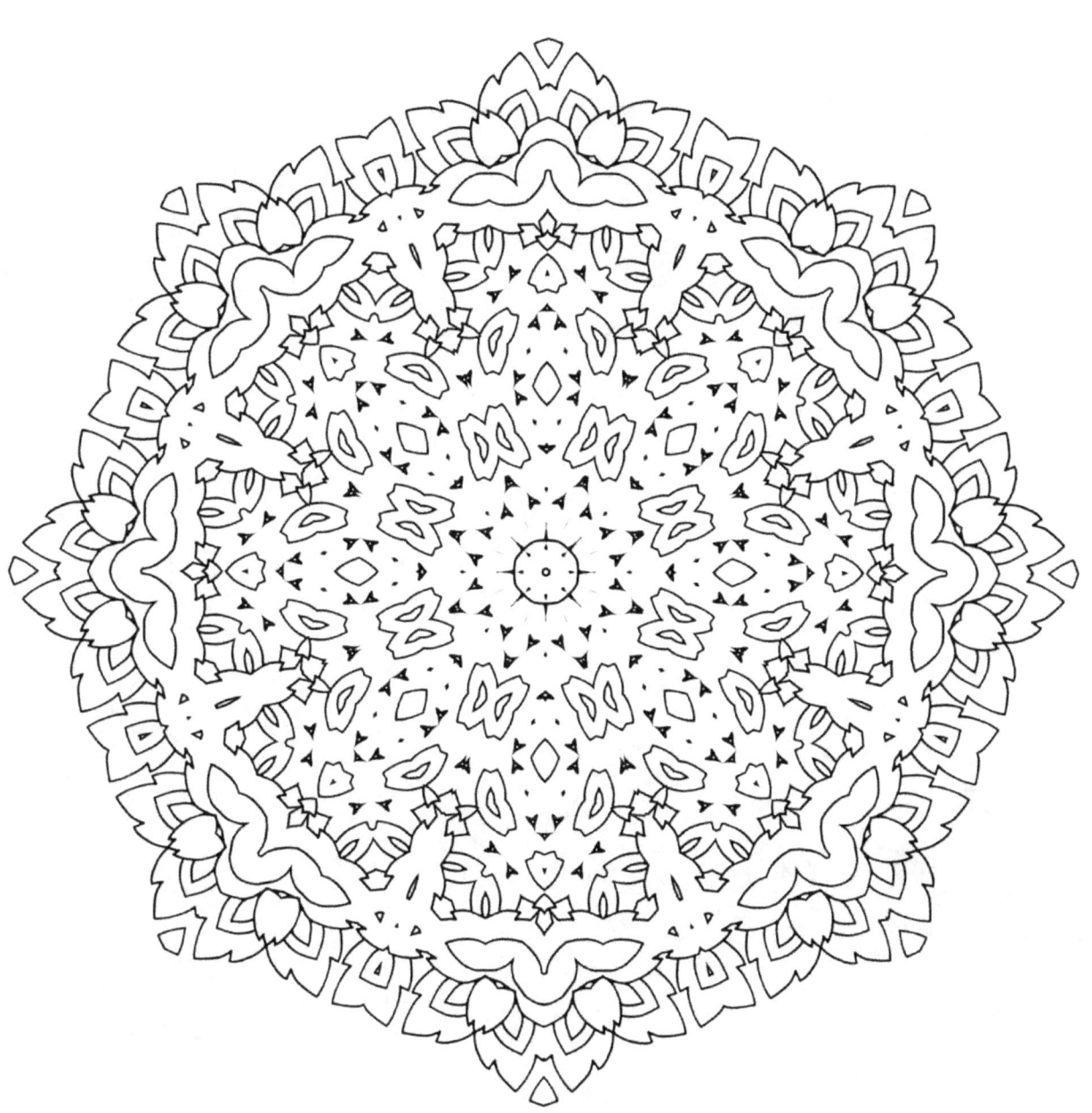

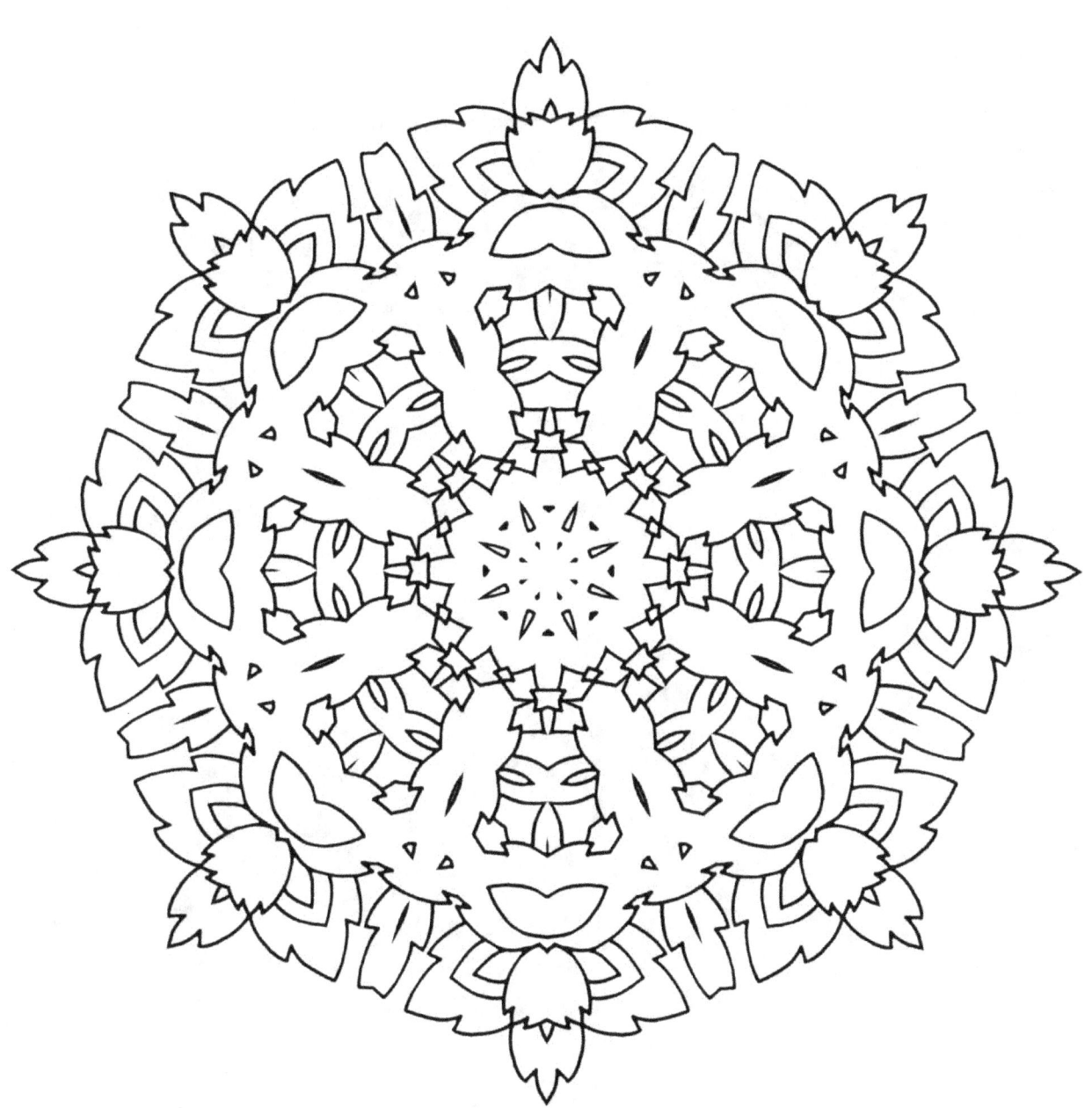

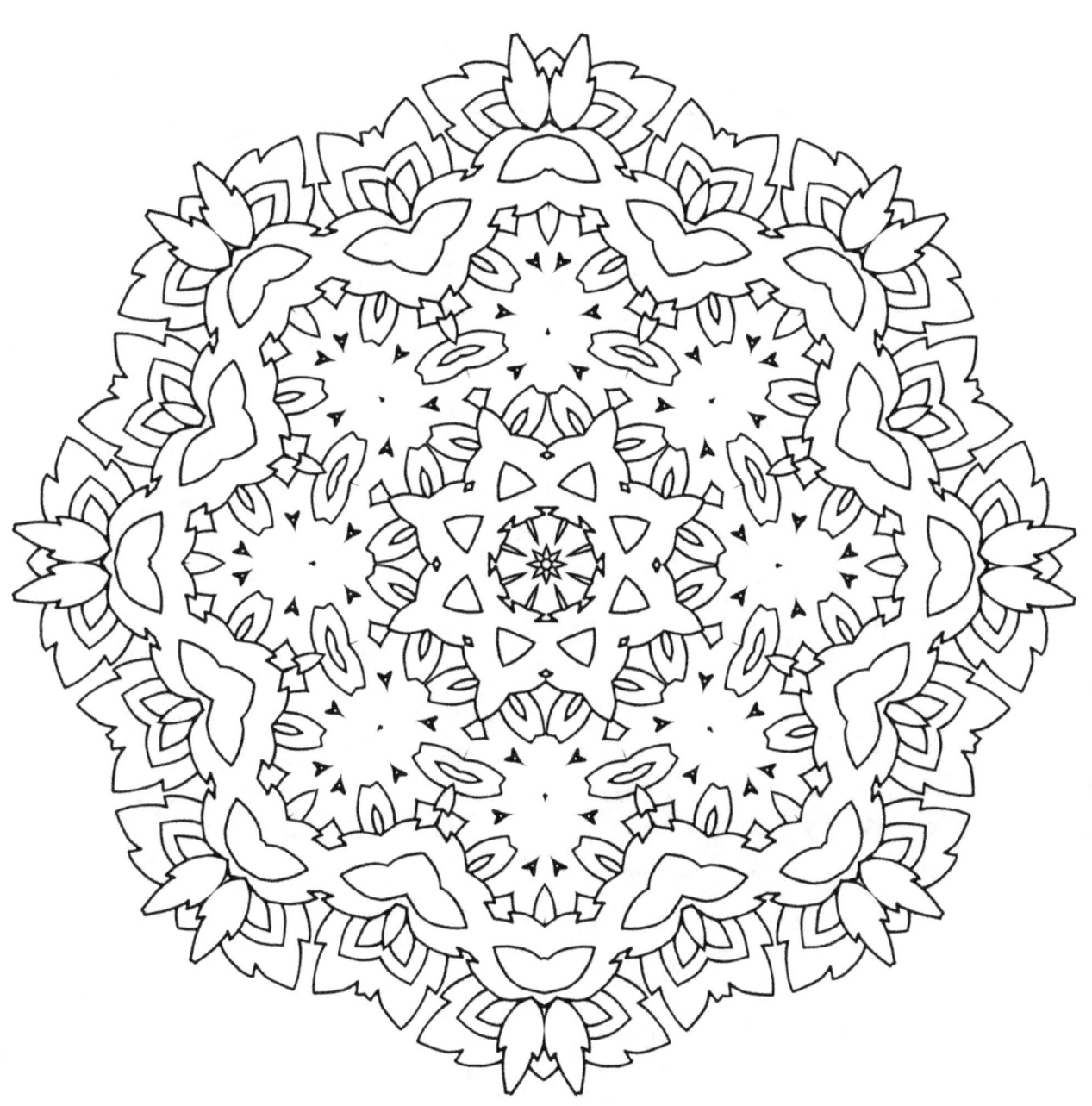

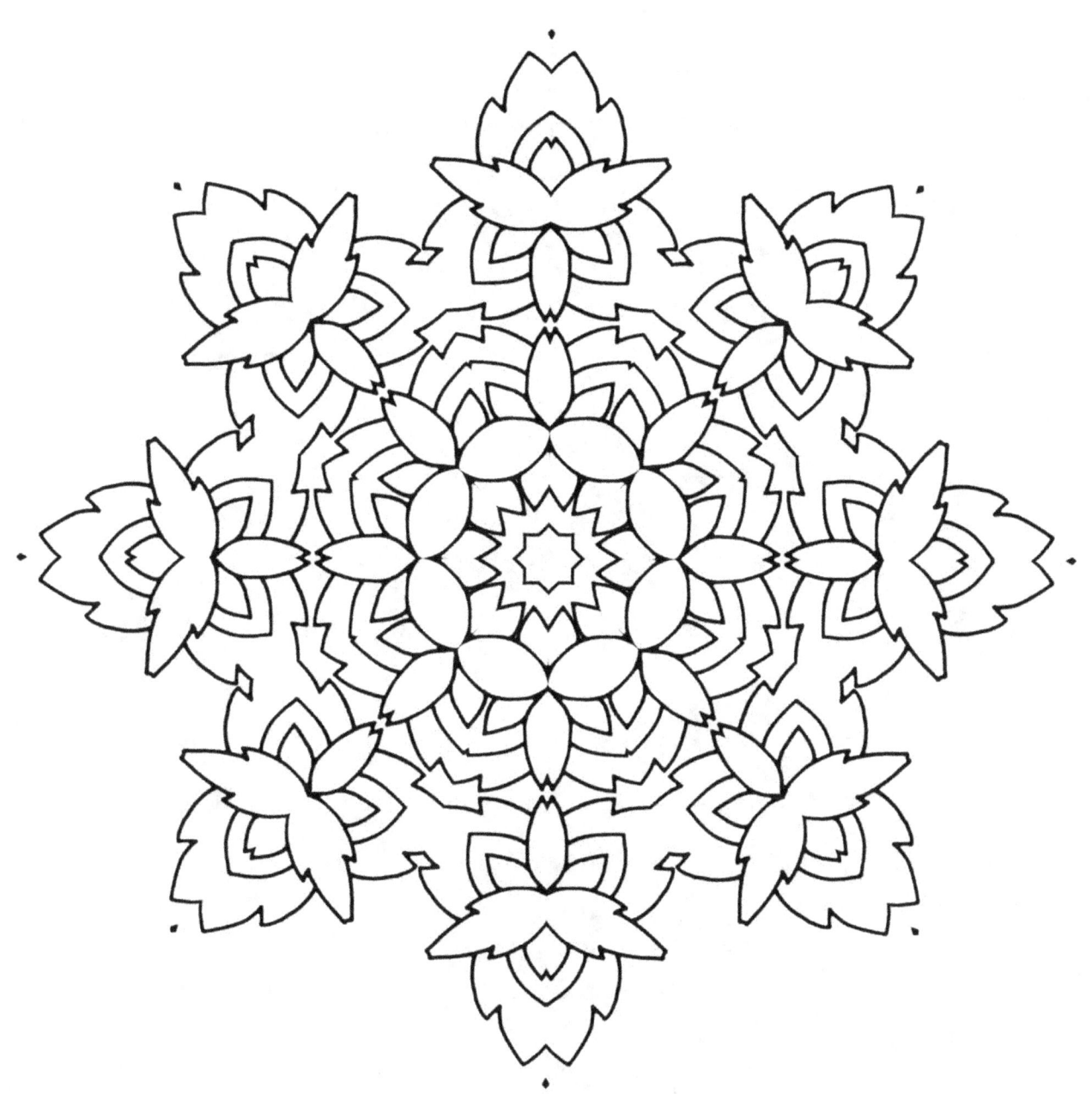

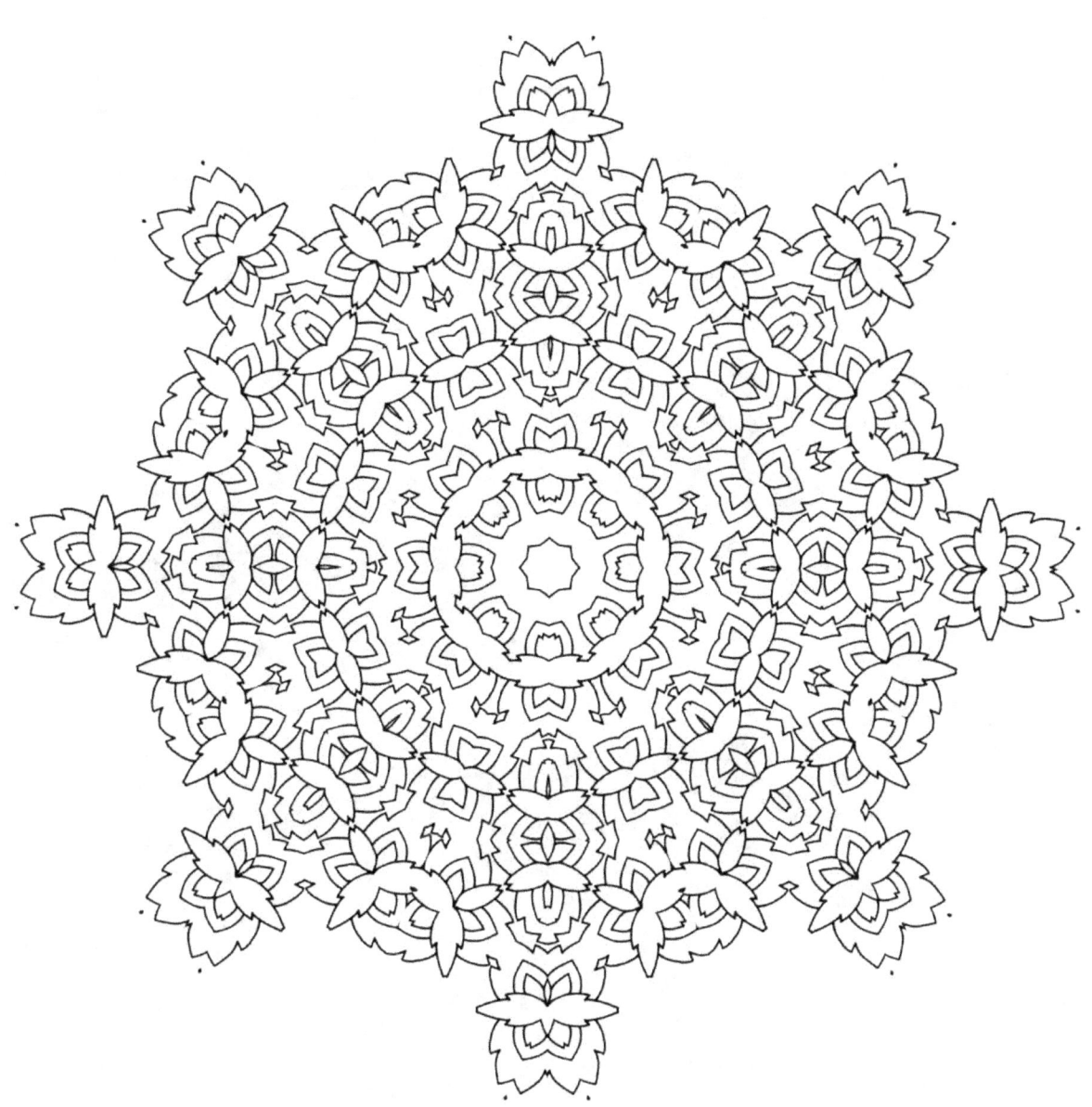

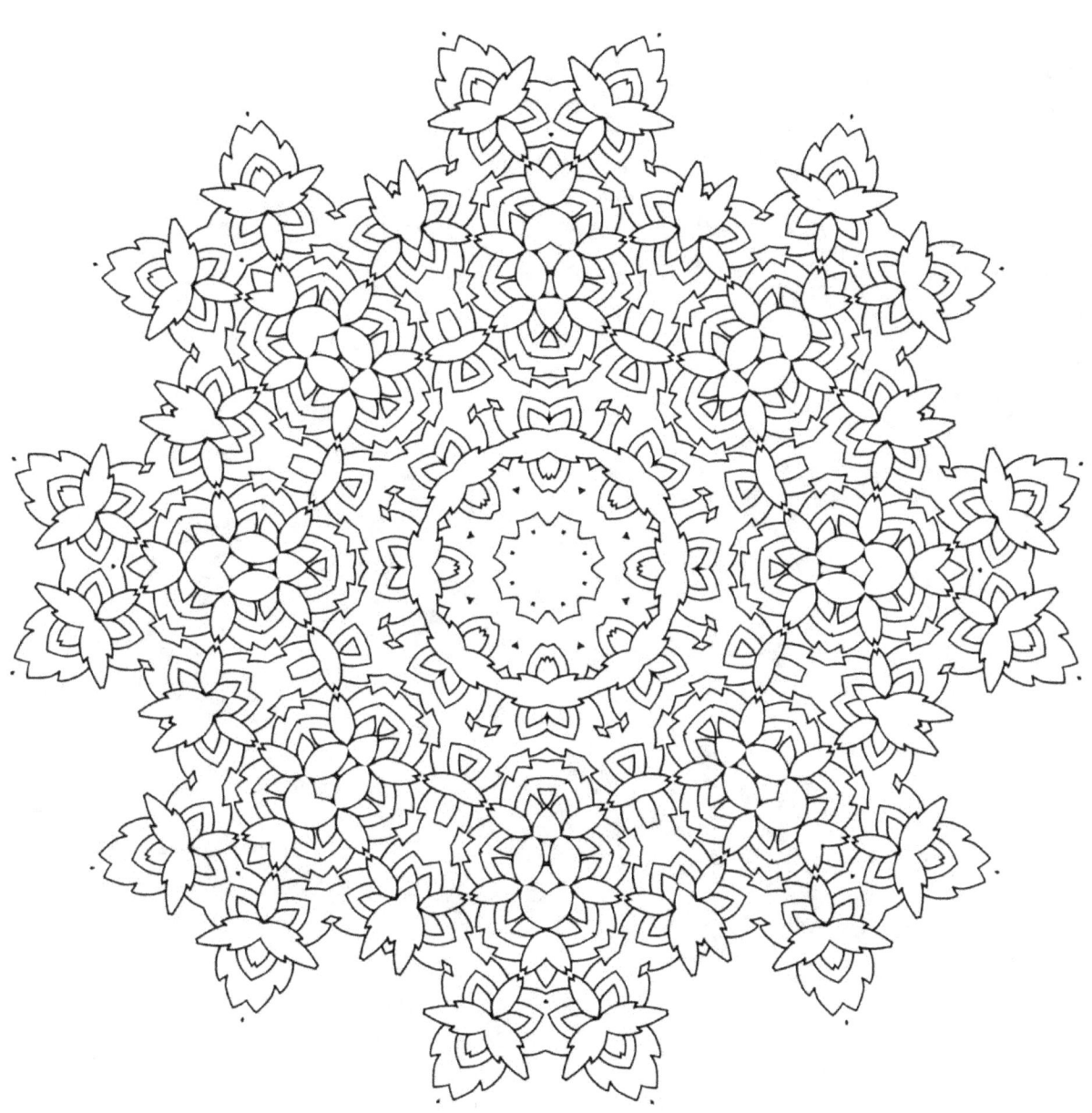

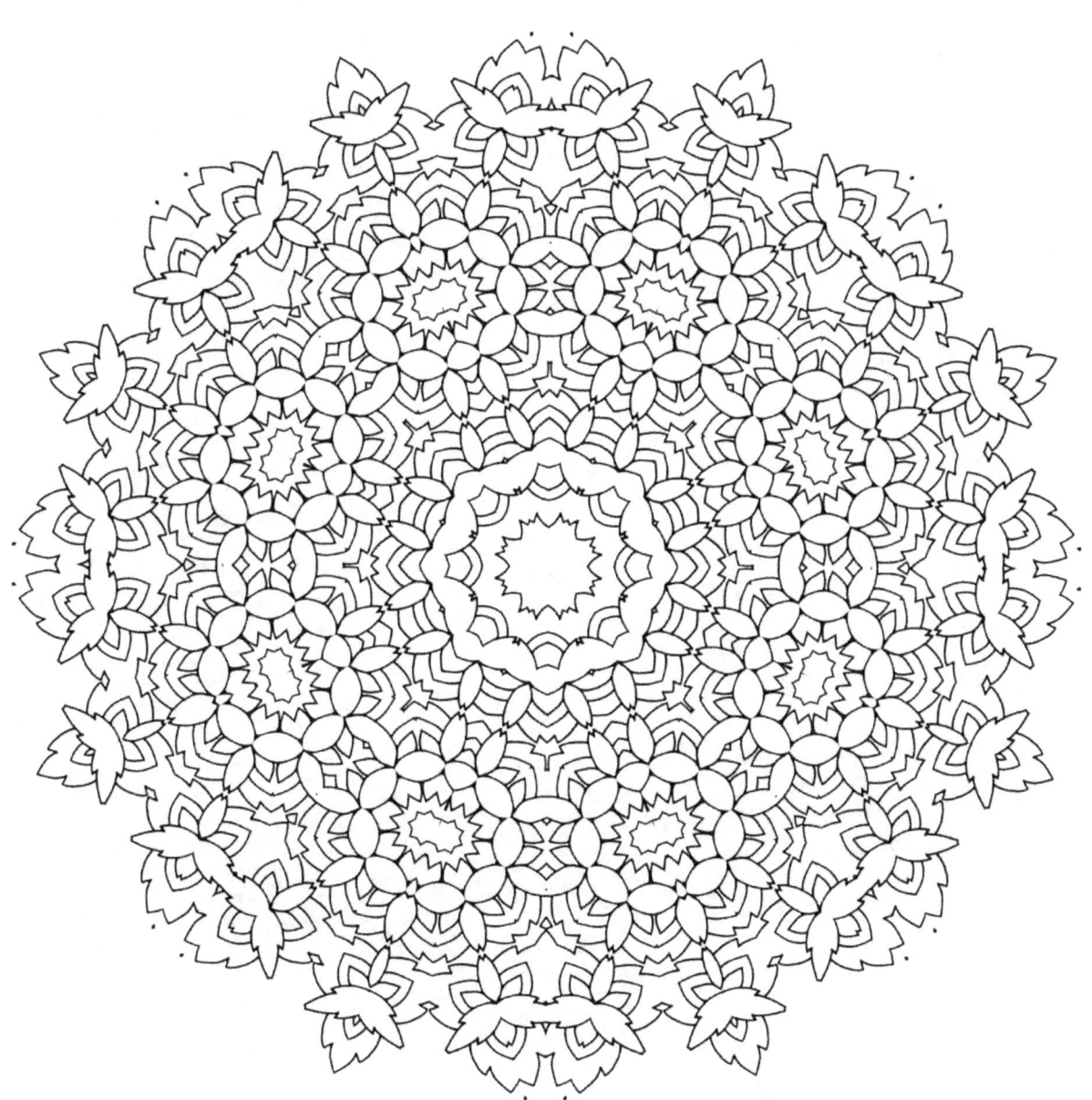

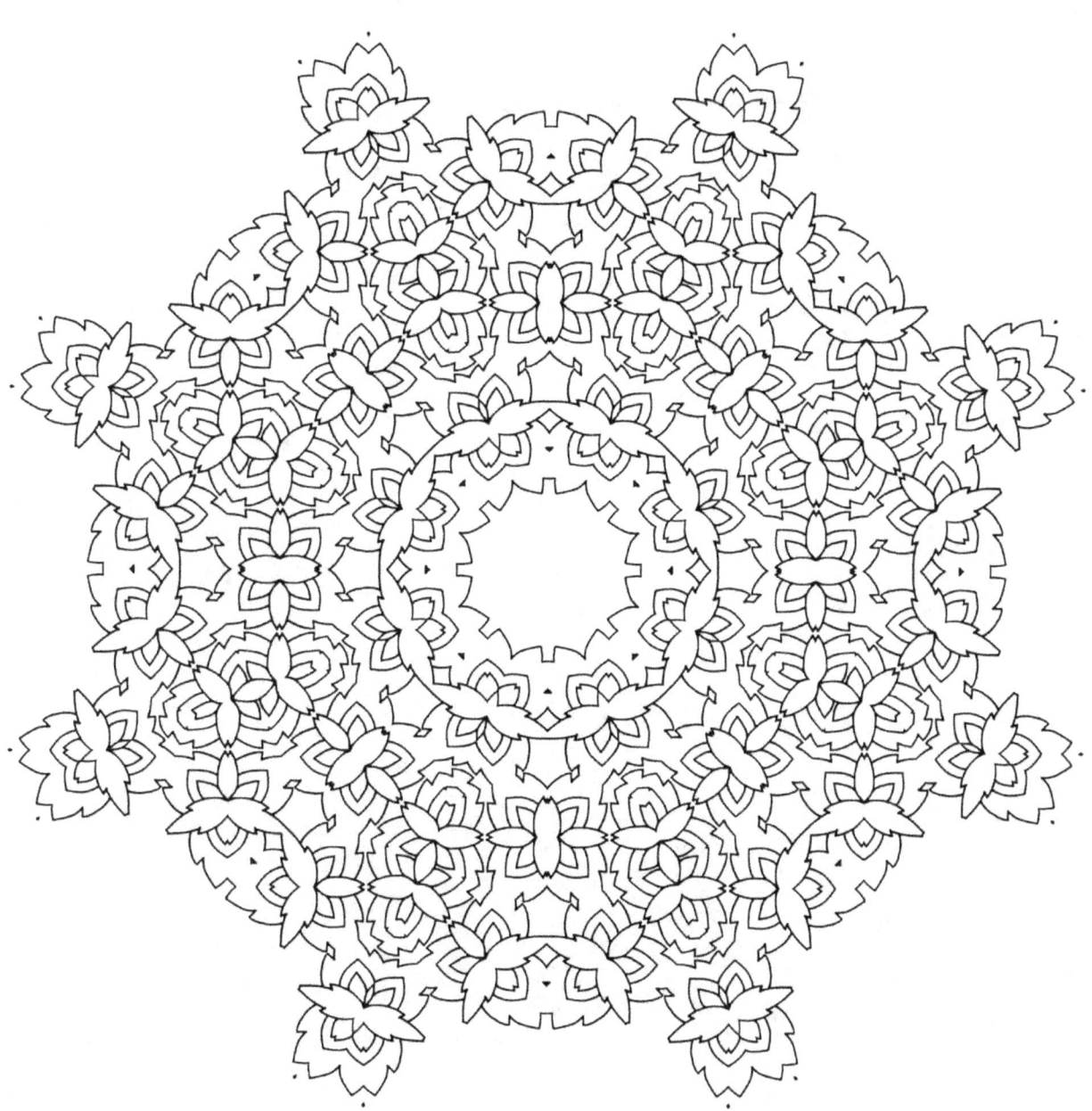

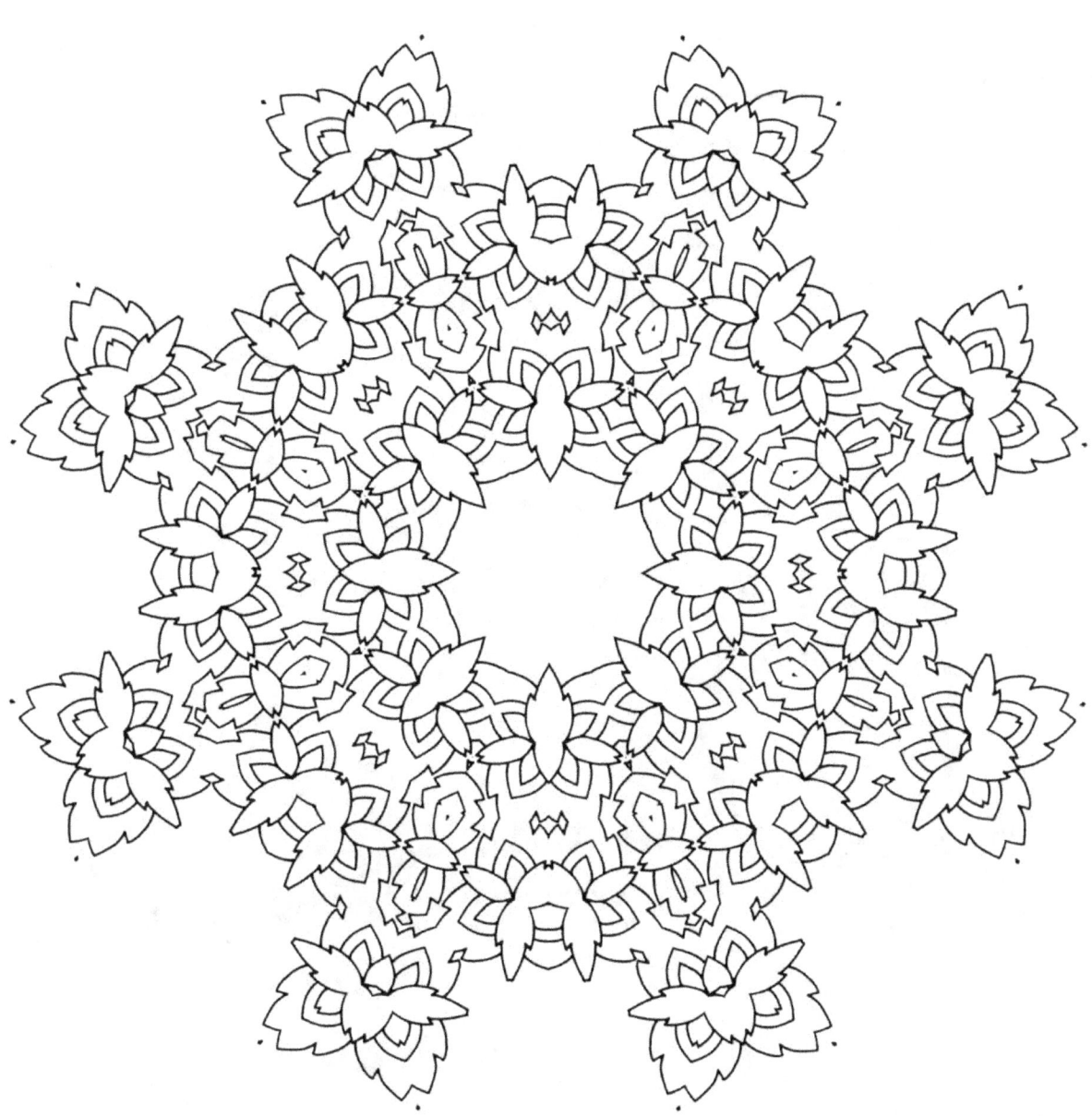

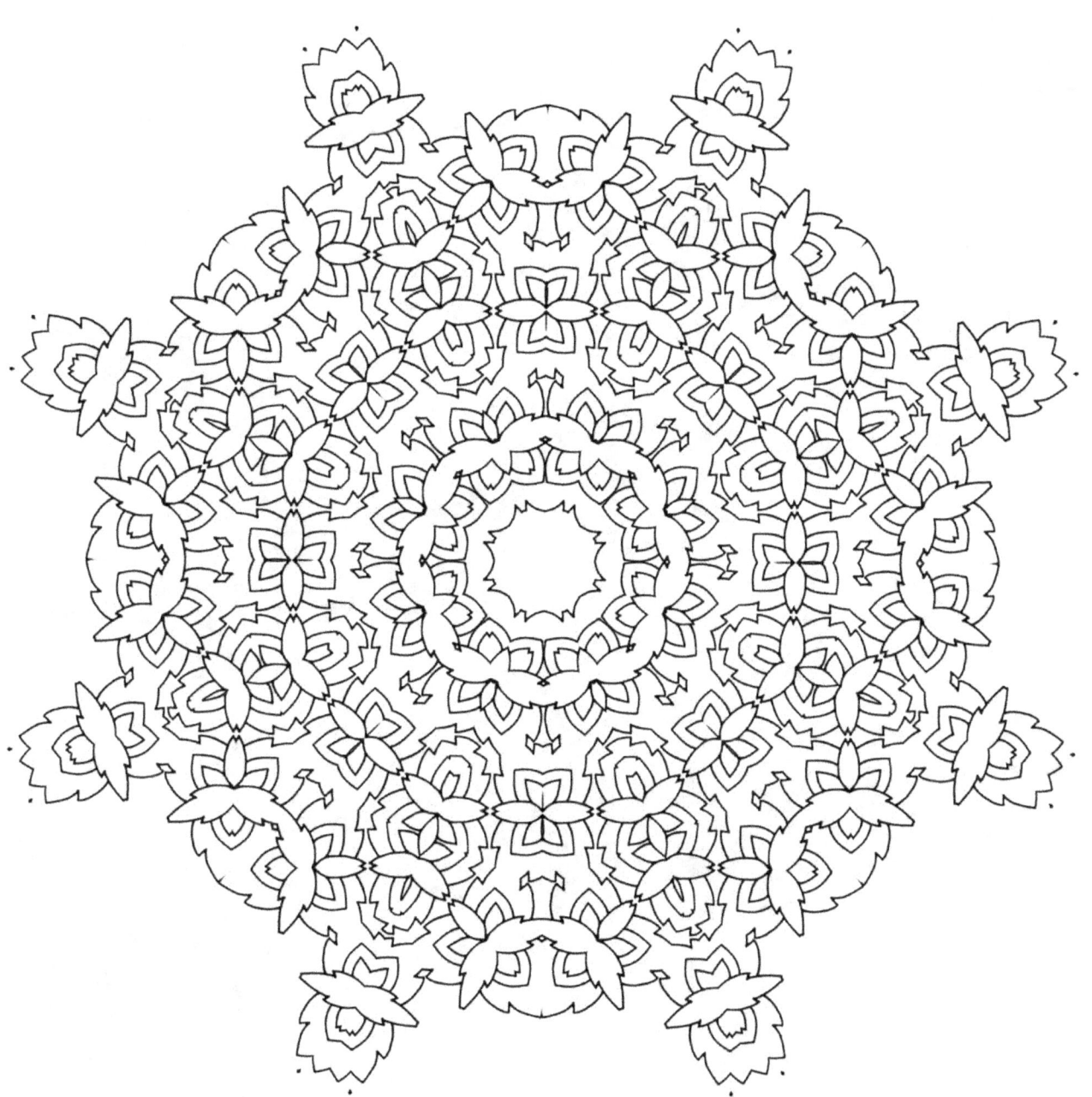

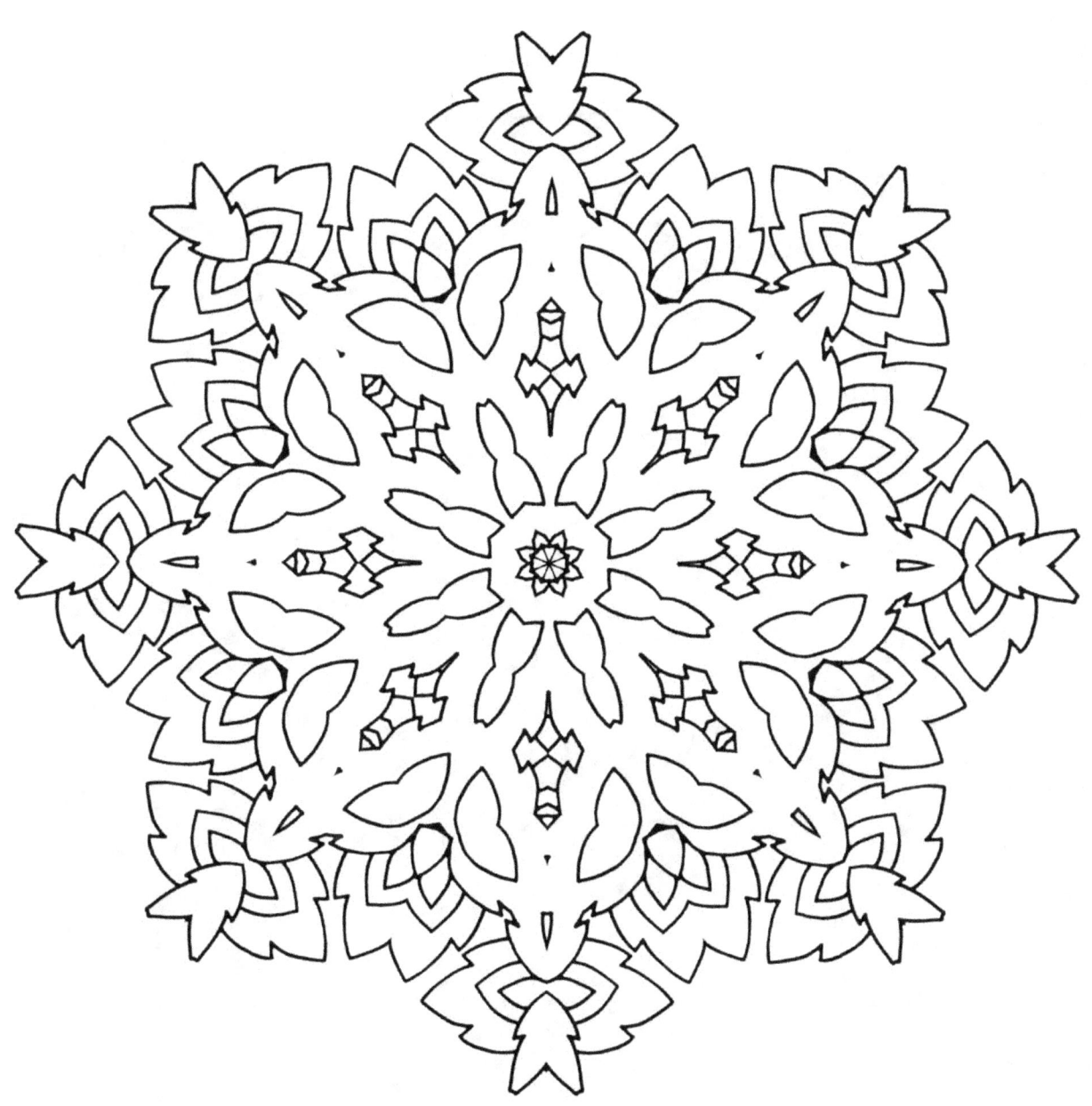

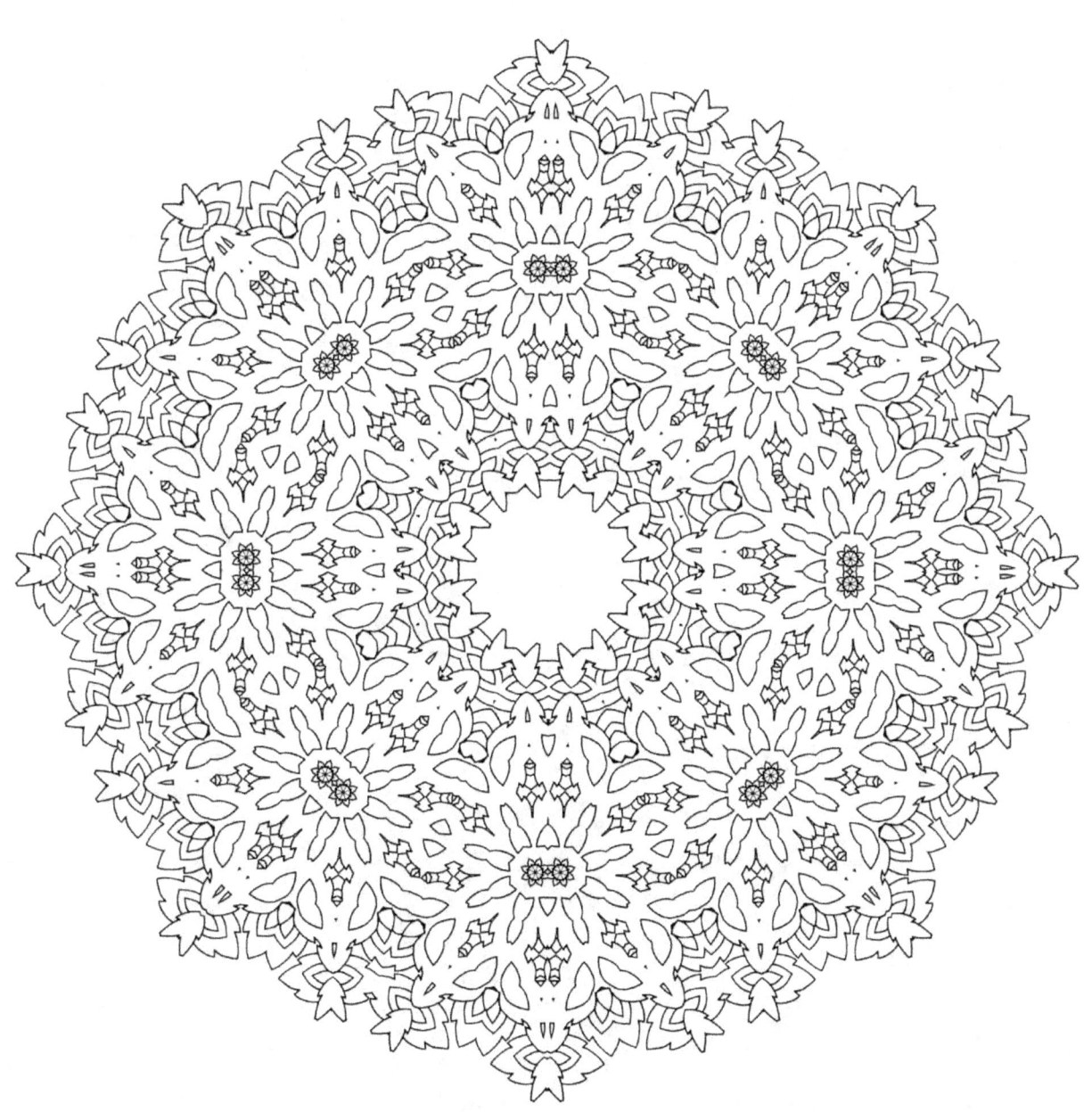

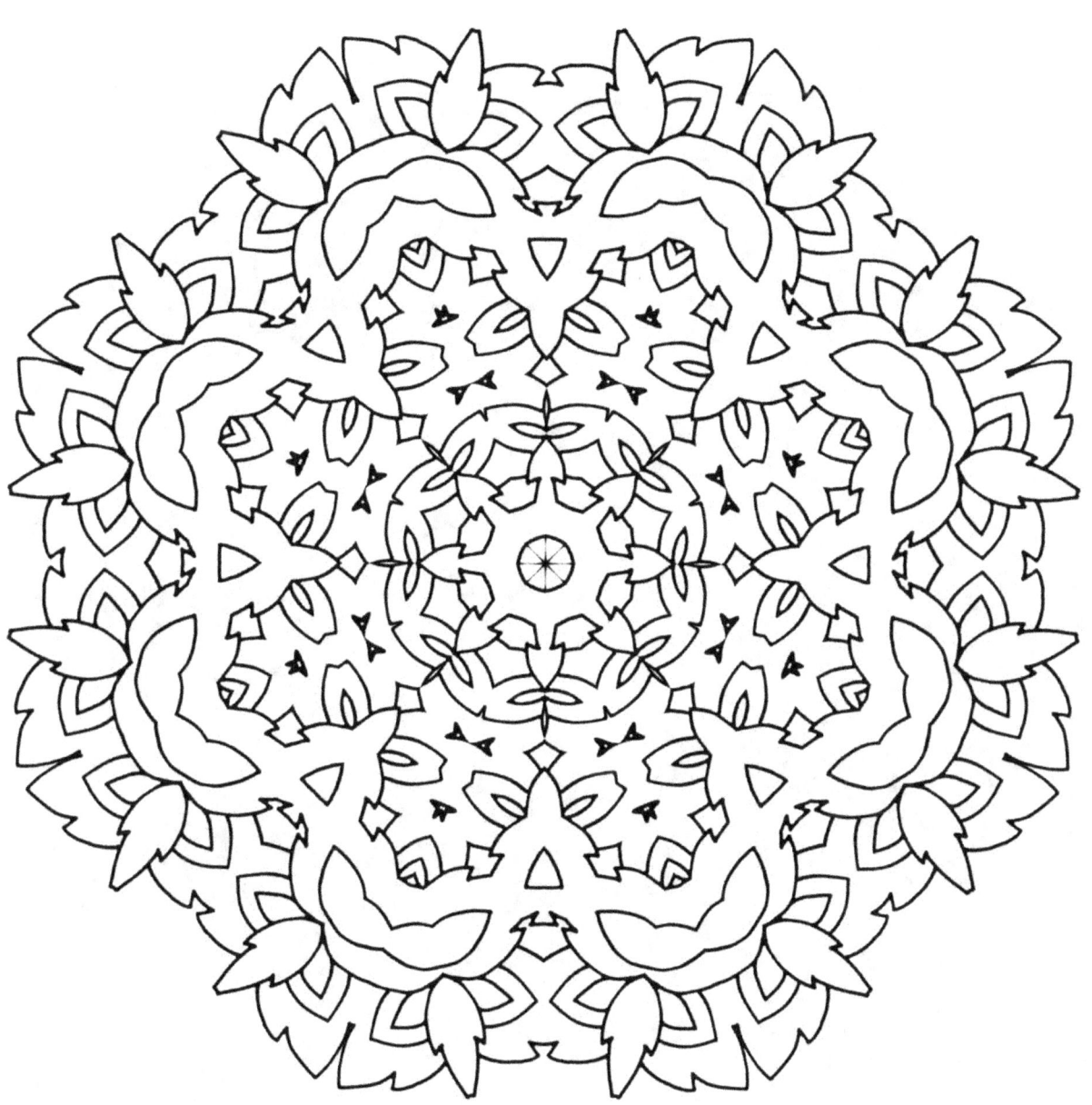

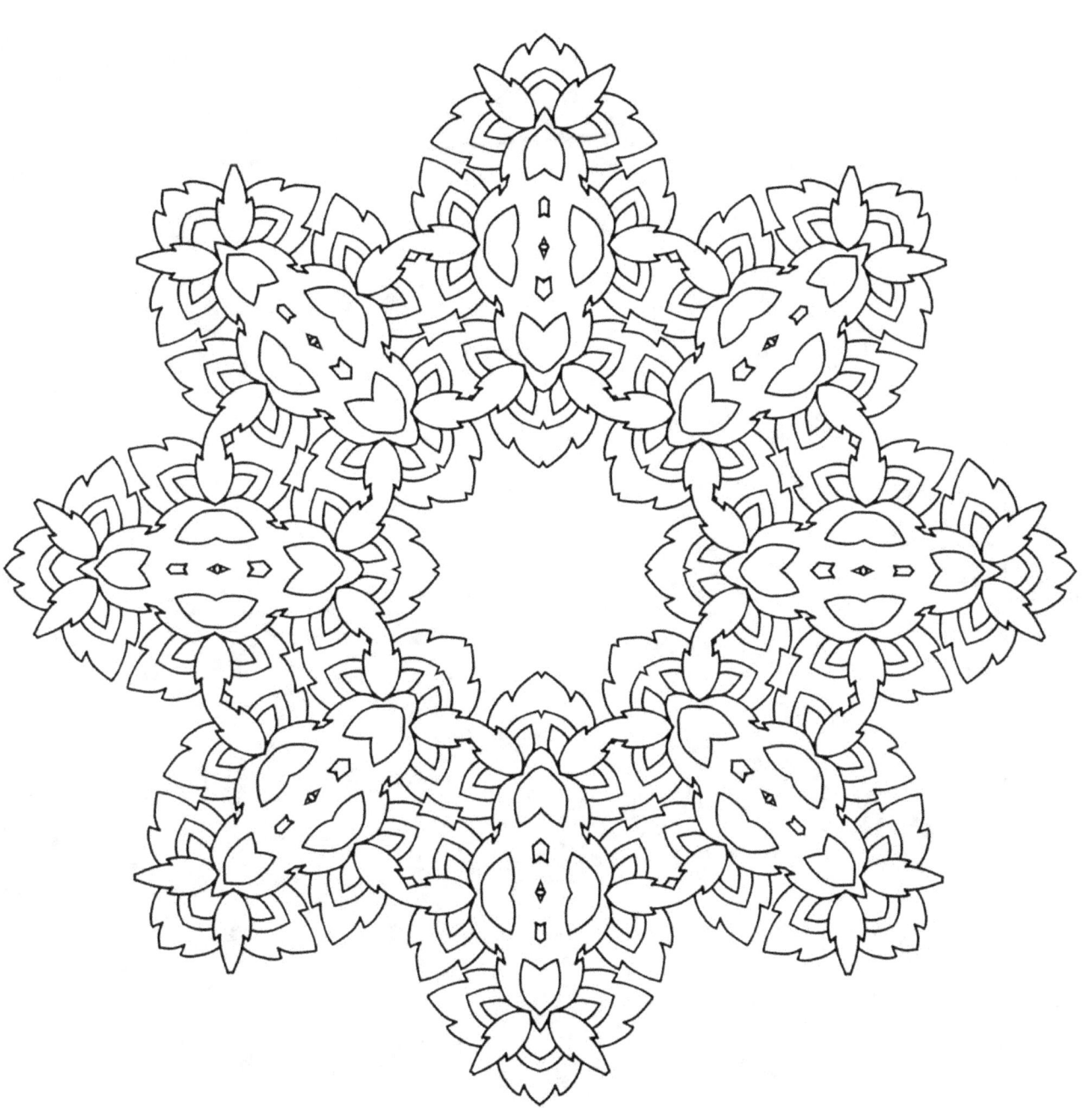

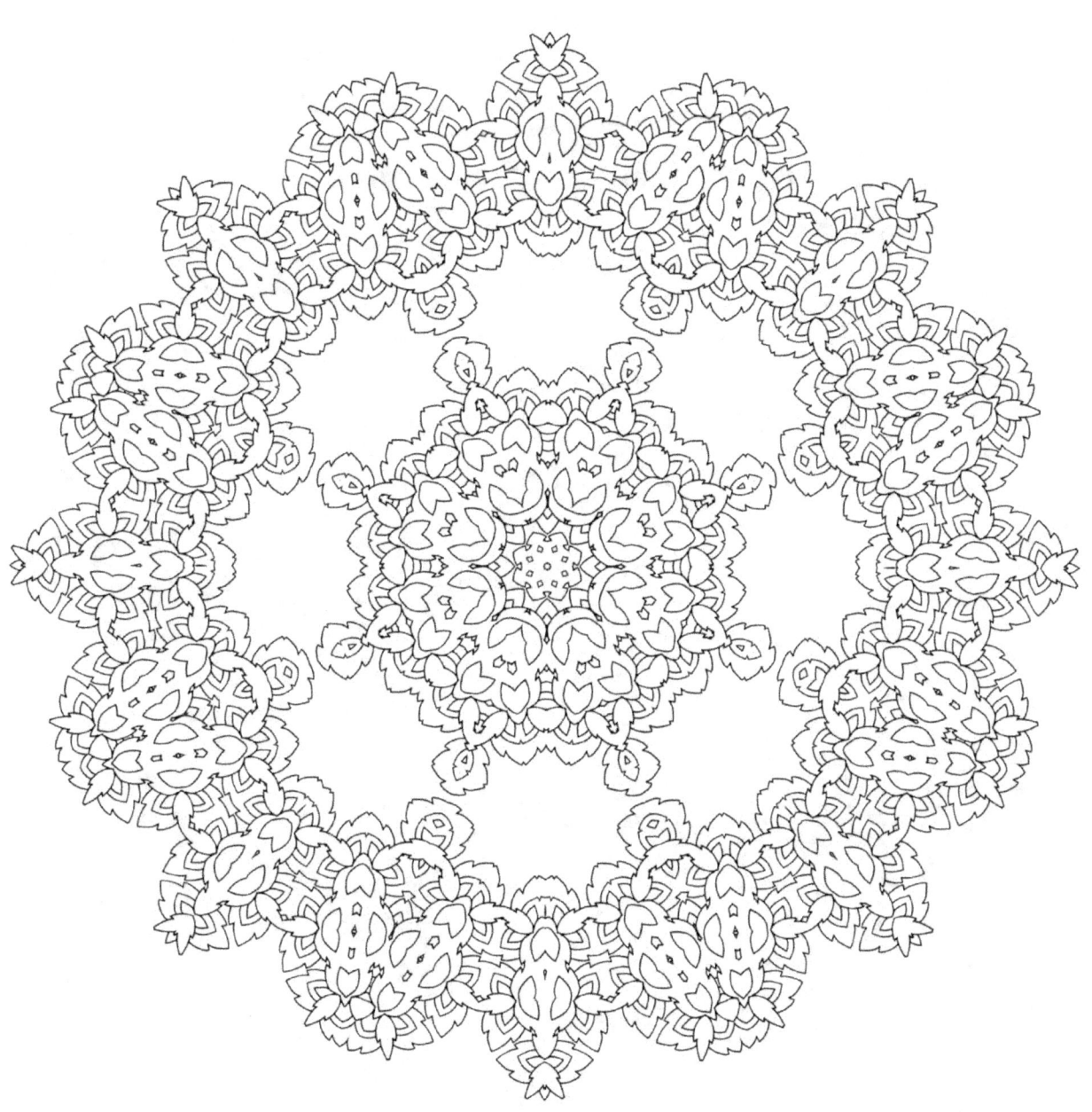

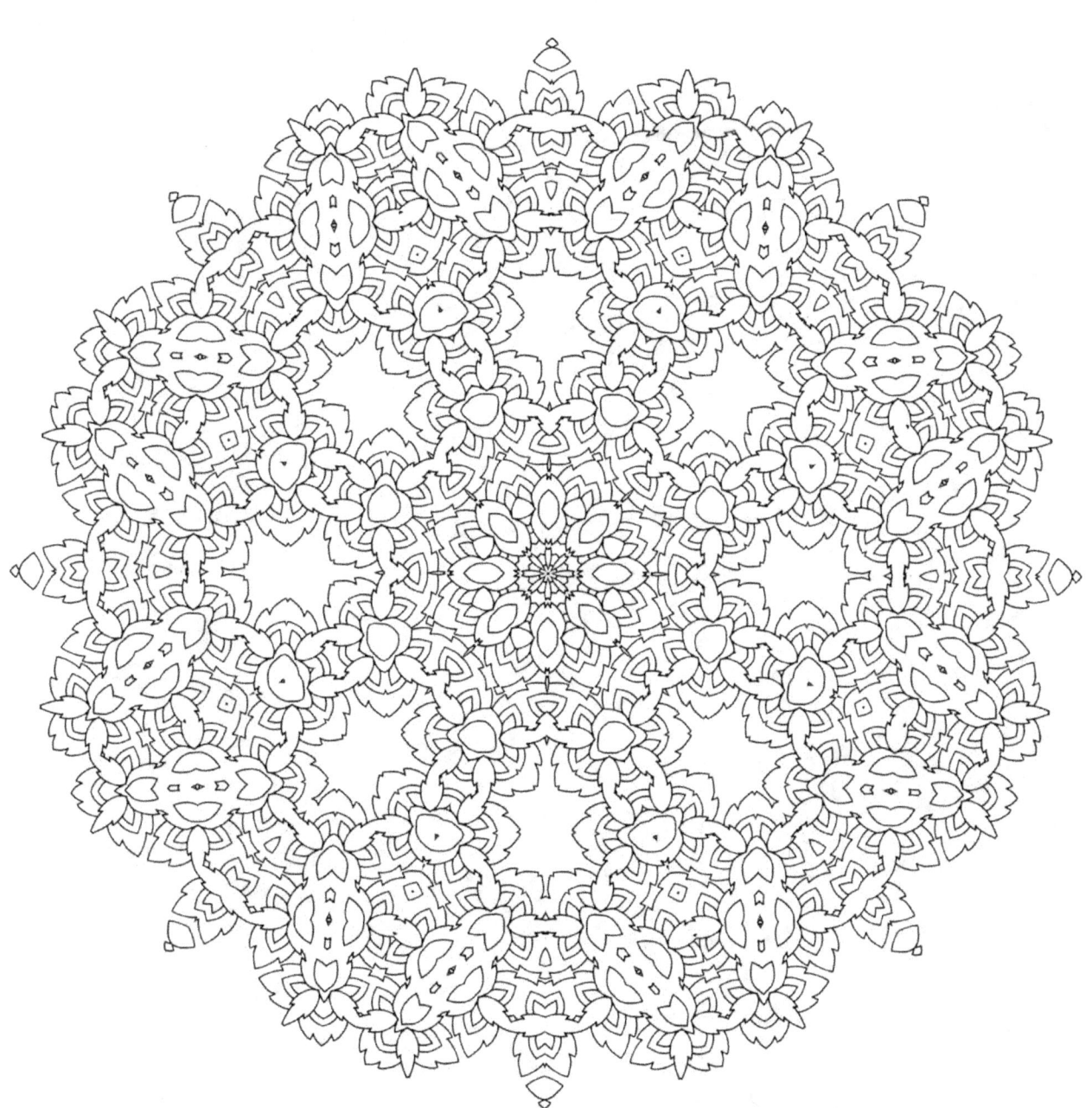

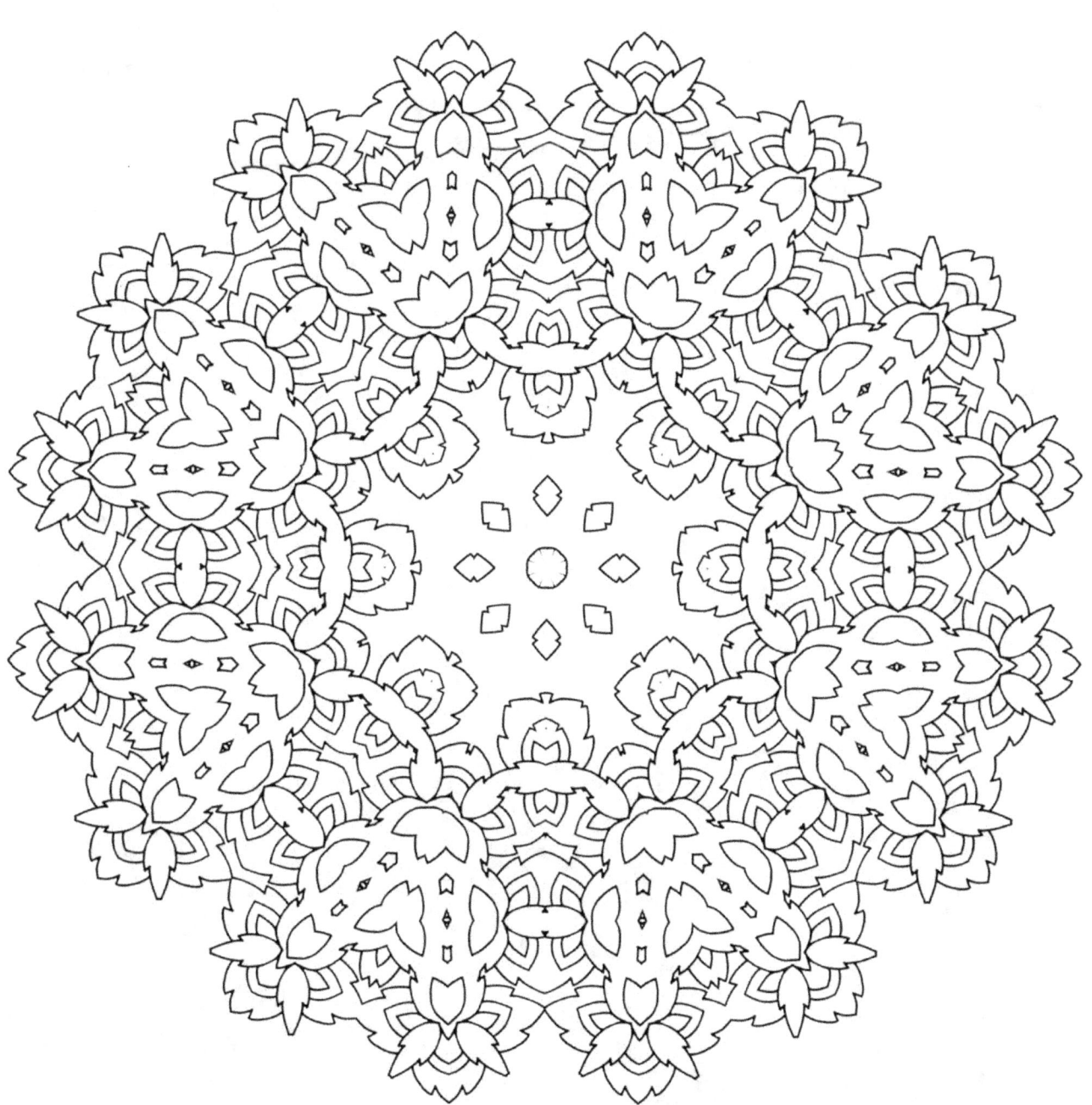

# Thank you

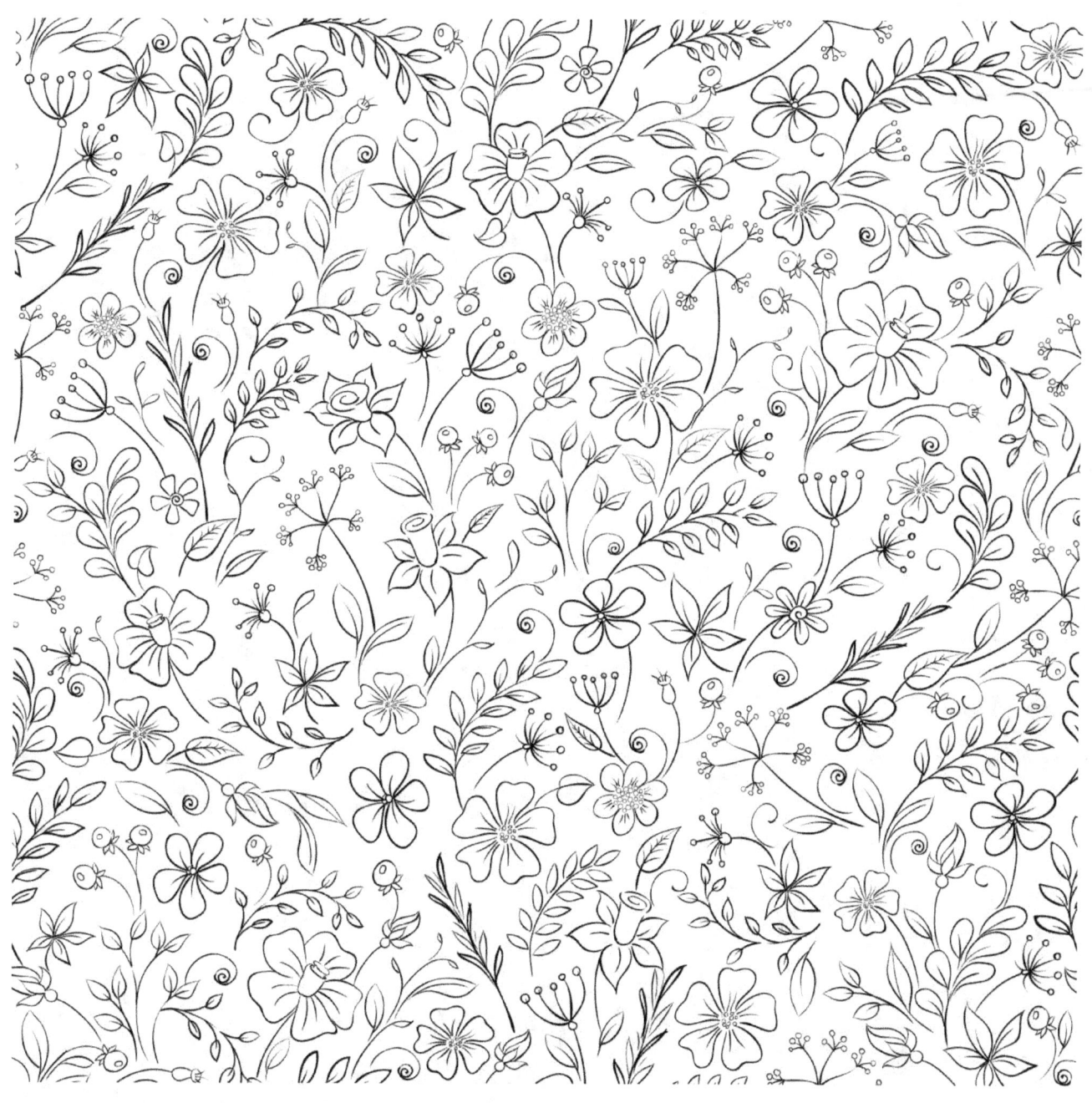

www.ingramcontent.com/pod-product-compliance
Lightning Source LLC
Chambersburg PA
CBHW081603220526
45468CB00010B/2758